Social Anxiety

Discover How to Quiet Your Negative Thoughts, Overcome Worry, Build Your Social Skills, and Cure Shyness so You Can Have Small Talk with Ease Even as an Introvert

Social Anxiety

Discover How to Quiet Your Negative Thoughts, Overcome Worry, Build Your Social Skills, and Cure Shyness so You Can Have Small Talk with Ease Even as an Introvert

Contents

Introduction

The times we're living in are unprecedented in many ways, and yet, deep down, we have hardly changed for thousands of years. What this means is that our lifestyle, technology, and many other things that shape our days have, in a way, surpassed us. Modern living certainly provides many comforts and perks; still, we often find ourselves naturally unequipped to deal with some of the challenges that these new ways of life have brought with them.

Some of the problems that used to be a freak occurrence - and only bothered particularly unfortunate individuals - are now becoming more commonplace. These problems include numerous forms of personality disorders and other mental health concerns, one of which is social anxiety. It is a sad and strange irony that social anxiety is an increasingly common problem in a time when our means of communication are more advanced and accessible than ever - *and when the world is interconnected like never before.*

Indeed, many folks from all walks of life seem to struggle with social interaction nowadays, so you're far from being alone. Social interaction is one of the critical aspects of the human experience, which is why social anxiety can not only deprive you of pleasant moments but also make your professional life suffer significantly. Folks who don't have such problems might not even realize it, but social interaction permeates a normal human life as few other things do. Getting even the most menial of tasks done can entail interaction, and when that becomes difficult, life can really take a downward turn.

Seeing as we are such social animals by nature, social skills are also one of the more important predictors of success. It's no secret that those who are adept at social situations tend to get ahead in many areas of life, especially when it comes to career opportunities and romantic prospects. Overall, social skills are one of the most critical areas to improve for a more fulfilled life.

The objective of this book is to help you do exactly that. If you have experience with social anxiety or suspect that you might, this book will teach you precisely what this disorder is and how it works, but also how you can mend the problem. Indeed, even though it's a complex issue that's still being researched, social anxiety is something that you can fight on your own, with moderate to great success.

It's important to understand that you are only one of many people with this problem and that there's nothing inherently wrong with you. Social anxiety can have numerous causes, but the cure is almost always the same or very similar. In the simplest possible terms, the issue revolves around a skill that you've lost and will have to master again. In the process, you will also master yourself.

By the end of this book, you will have a better understanding of what this disorder truly is, but you will also know much more about how exactly your brain works, particularly in relation to social anxiety. You will learn to differentiate between social anxiety and some other normal psychological processes or personality traits like introversion, fear, or plain old shyness.

While it's not a substitute for professional psychiatric help and therapy, this book contains up-to-date information and proven methods to overcome your anxiety. It will also help you on your journey toward greater self-development and awareness, both of which are important for achieving long-lasting peace of mind. In the process of overcoming your anxiety, you will become a more confident individual and will learn valuable skills in communication.

No matter how many bad experiences you've had and however hopeless your situation might feel, you are not beyond help. As you will find in this book, beating your social anxiety might be difficult, and it might feel like an uphill battle at times, which is why you'll need patience and perseverance, on top of a desire to get better. Nonetheless, it is a battle that every person has the strength to win. That strength must be unlocked, though, and this book will eventually help you do that. Without further ado, we will begin by looking at what social anxiety really is and where we are at when it comes to an understanding and treating this problem.

Chapter One: What Is Social Anxiety?

It is important to state that social anxiety is not merely shyness or introversion, although they might often correlate. Social anxiety is a diagnosed personality disorder, generally referred to as social anxiety disorder, or SAD for short. Social anxiety was formerly known as social phobia, which is a term that's still sometimes used. In the simplest terms, social anxiety is a sort of fear of social situations that stems from a feeling of inadequacy and a fear of being scrutinized in some way.

Everyone can get nervous about certain situations, particularly when they are important. For instance, many people tend to get nervous before an important job interview, even if they don't really have a social anxiety disorder. And even though this nervousness usually comes from the fear of scrutiny that a job interview will inevitably entail, it's still not social anxiety disorder *by definition*. Social anxiety implies a particularly intense and irrational fear that can completely cloud your mind and occurs automatically - even when you can't rationally identify what it is about a situation that scares you. The irrationality and intensity of the fearful reaction that social anxiety entails are why it's sometimes referred to as a social phobia.

The fact that we have evolved to be social creatures is something that makes social anxiety particularly tragic and problematic. Even when we have such a disorder and when our fear makes us think that we don't want to get into social situations, our minds still subtly crave the interaction and the contact. Prolonged isolation and a lack of intimacy or any social contact, however meaningful or not, can have dramatic consequences on our mental health, regardless of how sociable or unsociable, we think we are.

Of course, therefore, social anxiety often leads to feelings of loneliness and alienation. As you might know from experience, this is a difficult situation to be in because it feels like an awfully paradoxical trap where one loathes the prospect of getting into a social situation but feels the same way about their loneliness in the meantime. As such, a social anxiety disorder can lead to all sorts of complications when it comes to mental or even physical health, depending on the case. That's if the disorder is left unchecked, of course.

If you have only a moderate problem with social anxiety, you should certainly try to nip it in the bud. At this time, you might think that it only affects your social life and makes it difficult to make friends, but, over time, social anxiety can make many other areas of your life difficult, as we mentioned. If the problem can grow, you can find yourself going from feeling discomfort at a party to having your career stifled, or worse.

Seeing as it can have such far-reaching consequences for the quality of life and productivity of individuals, it's no surprise that social anxiety disorder is something that's of great concern for society. SAD (social anxiety disorder) is just one of the numerous forms of anxiety disorders that pose a problem, particularly in the West. In the United States, anxiety disorders affect some 40 million adults, making such disorders the most common form of mental health issue. On a yearly basis, around one-fifth of adult Americans will report being affected by some form of anxiety.

The incidence of social anxiety disorder is around 7% of the adult population in the US. This statistic includes mild to severe cases of social anxiety, but it only accounts for individuals with a prolonged problem. Folks who are affected by SAD for shorter periods of time are even more numerous. Since it affects millions of people, social anxiety has its cost for the economy as well, just like other forms of anxiety. Because it's a growing problem across the board, social anxiety now receives significant attention, and we understand it much better than we used to.

Symptoms

Social anxiety – a diagnosed disease - comes with a range of identifiable symptoms that can be used to determine if the issue is SAD or if it is something else. Of course, the symptoms of social anxiety are mostly like those of other forms of anxiety disorders, while the main difference is in the triggers that bring those symptoms. The symptoms can generally be divided into emotional or behavioral symptoms and physical symptoms.

Indeed, when it strikes, social anxiety can interfere with the way you behave in certain situations and how you feel both physically and emotionally. However, when it comes to behavior, social anxiety has long-term, persistent symptoms and signs as well. It alters one's lifestyle, habits, plans, and eventually, even life outcomes. When it comes to the behavioral and emotional side of things, below are some of the common symptoms and signs of social anxiety disorder:

- Excessive fear of judgment and social situations that might lead to it
- The fear of communicating with strangers
- Obsessing over the possibility of embarrassing yourself or being publically humiliated
- The fear of anxiety itself or, rather, of others noticing the problem or its physical symptoms that you might be experiencing
- The fear of attracting the attention of others, especially in groups or crowds

- Persistent and sometimes growing anxiety in anticipation of an upcoming social situation that you're aware of in advance
- Adjusting plans and canceling activities to avoid triggers, even at the detriment to your social or professional life
- Ceasing to partake in activities that used to bring you pleasure and joy, simply for fear of social situations and the anxiety they bring
- Obsessive posthoc analysis of every detail of interaction after it has ended, with a focus on how you performed during its course
- An inability to focus on the other party in a conversation, instead of obsessing over your own appearance and behavior
- An excessively negative outlook on future social scenarios and their consequences

Because of all these issues, folks with social anxiety tend to struggle with starting conversations, participating in group activities, meeting strangers, dating, maintaining eye contact, visiting a store, or even using a public restroom. When an outbreak of social anxiety occurs, you will usually notice the following symptoms:

- An increased heart rate - *sometimes, severely so*
- Trembling
- Stress sweating
- Nausea
- Blushing
- Trouble breathing, which can make it difficult to speak as well
- Dizziness
- An overall loss of control over your thoughts and a feeling of panic

If you tend to experience any or all these symptoms in social situations and are made to feel very uncomfortable because of it, this is a good indication that you're struggling with a social anxiety disorder.

Diagnosis and Complications

As we mentioned, social anxiety disorder has been taken seriously by mainstream psychiatry and psychology for quite a while now, especially in the developed world. As such, it is a disorder that can be diagnosed with great accuracy. Analyzing the symptoms after they have occurred and been observed is one way of diagnosis, but experts have also developed useful questionnaires and personality tests that can evaluate whether you have SAD and how severe it might be.

If you decide to talk to a professional in order to confirm beyond any doubt whether you have a social anxiety disorder, you might be asked to talk about past symptoms or take a questionnaire. The questionnaires usually consist of statements that you are supposed to agree or disagree with. Such tests can vary in complexity, but their core idea is to get insight into the way you react to certain situations and how your mind works. The results will then help determine whether you are socially anxious - and to what degree.

In addition to considering the symptoms and signs we have already discussed, you can also take such tests and quizzes on your own. There are all sorts of quizzes that you can find on the Internet, some more detailed and reliable than others. Still, the most accurate diagnosis will require consulting with a professional who will be able to consider all the particularities of your individual case.

If left unchecked, a social anxiety disorder can evolve in many ways and lead to complications, especially when it comes to your overall mental health. In time, your social anxiety can take charge of every aspect of your life, dictating everything you do and how or when you do it. Socially anxious people often end up with diminished self-esteem and, of course, abysmal social skills. These problems are especially likely when the onset of the disorder is during the teenage years, which is an important developmental stage. Unfortunately, this scenario is all too common when it comes to SAD, and kids can thus miss out on developing crucial social skills and confidence that will come into play later in life.

Social anxiety can make people fragile and irritable, unable to handle criticism or even take friendly advice. Folks with SAD tend to be much less assertive as well, which hinders professional and academic performance. As the disorder pushes the individual further into isolation, all sorts of other problems can come up. It's not uncommon for socially anxious individuals to end up with major depressive disorder and many other mental issues that can even lead to suicide – or, at least, attempts of it. Of course, many sufferers will also resort to self-medicating with alcohol or drugs, which, in turn, can lead to substance abuse and a whole plethora of other problems that go along with that.

Causes and Risk Factors

As is often the case with these things, the causes of social anxiety disorder can vary, and they are worth discussion. Overall, social anxiety disorder stems from biological or environmental factors or a combination of both. It has been observed that social anxiety is often inherited, but it's unclear whether this heritability stems from genetics or nurture and learned behavior. It's certainly possible that social anxiety, like other mental problems, can be passed down through genes, but this is still debated.

As for the brain itself, it has been suggested that the party responsible for the fearful and anxious reaction is the amygdala. When this part of the brain is abnormally active, which is the case in some people, social anxiety tends to be a problem.

When it comes to the environmental factors that might cause the disorder, they are plentiful. Past experiences can play an important role, particularly negative social experiences. They can be especially affecting if they occur when one is very young or otherwise vulnerable. Of course, parents can also be the inadvertent culprits either by setting an example with their own anxious behavior or by being overprotective or not properly socializing their child during the formative years. As for direct mistreatment or child abuse, it's unclear if such experiences in childhood can lead to social anxiety, although they are certainly connected to other problems.

Apart from the murky and debated subject of underlying causes, there are also risk factors to consider, all of which can imply a higher risk of developing SAD at some point in life. Apart from family history and the parental influence we mentioned, environmental risk factors for children also include experiences like bullying, excessive teasing, humiliation, and failure to make friends. Such experiences can lead to withdrawal and alienation, greatly contributing to subsequent social anxiety. Children who exhibit traits like shyness and a lack of sociability early in their lives should be worked with to reduce their elevated risk of developing SAD.

In the unfortunate cases where people have a condition or an appearance problem that attracts attention, the risk of social anxiety is higher as well. This includes many things that can make us self-conscious and turn social interaction into a chore, even if the people we interact with are kind to us. One of the most common problems of this kind is acne. Acne's onset during teenage years often correlates with the emergence of social anxiety, and it can certainly make things worse.

Treatment

Today, social anxiety is something that's treated with much success, and the chances are good that treatment options will get even better in the future. The two main approaches are cognitive-behavioral therapy – "CBT" for short - and medication. Of course, therapy will also often make use of both approaches, depending on the case in question.

Cognitive-behavioral therapy is an approach that focuses on the patient's thought patterns and other mental processes, considering how they affect anxiety. You will find later that this book's advice essentially constitutes CBT as well. It's simply the idea that by altering the patient's way of thinking via the use of counseling and personalized therapy, the patient can abandon thoughts and beliefs that lead to social anxiety. By changing thoughts and behavior, CBT truly addresses the root cause of the problem.

As its name suggests, CBT consists of two parts, wherein the cognitive part of the therapy deals with thoughts, and the behavioral half focuses on various activities. When it comes to CBT that's specific to social anxiety treatment, the cognitive part of the therapy tends to focus on replacing negative thoughts that trigger anxiety with positive ones. The behavioral component of the therapy often includes group therapy that involves activities that are meant to condition the patient to tolerate certain situations better gradually.

These activities tend to be those that have the potential to be at least somewhat uncomfortable for the patient, but it's a process of slow immunization, so to speak. Furthermore, group therapy activities provide an opportunity to put into practice the things a patient learns during cognitive therapy. This is one of the reasons why CBT is such a comprehensive and effective approach. CBT might also make use of relaxation techniques like meditation, mindfulness, and other approaches - many of which we will cover later in this book.

When it comes to meditation, if it's possible to treat the disorder without medication successfully, and although that's *ideal* (medication can indeed be very helpful), the medication that's used to treat social anxiety is what you would expect with other forms of anxiety as well, including benzodiazepines and SSRIs. The two main problems with medication are that they have side-effects and that they only treat the symptoms instead of addressing the *root cause.* That's why medication is only an additional tool to make the journey easier, not a long-term solution.

All in all, therapy for social anxiety has a great success rate, and in almost all cases, the problem is curable. Once the mind has been altered for the better and taught to look at things in a new light, the positive change is usually permanent. Often, all it takes is some willpower and patience on your part, as you'll see throughout this book.

Chapter Two: Social Anxiety, Shyness, and Introversion

In this chapter, we will go into more detail concerning the differences and connection between social anxiety and a couple of things that might resemble the disorder or accompany it but may also exist without SAD. First and foremost, it's important to understand that one's level of comfort in social situations, especially when we account for various personal preferences, can depend on many factors other than disorders or any kind of illness. Being a bit on the shy side is certainly a legitimate personality trait and not any kind of disorder.

Furthermore, being shy or anxious in certain social situations can be entirely natural, even for people who are otherwise never shy. Talking to a person you really like or being in a situation with strangers while noticing something sketchy going on can make anyone feel anxious and on edge. As you probably know, some people are also just naturally predisposed to being more outgoing and communicative than others, and sociability is certainly a spectrum. Understanding what shyness and introversion are, for instance, can be just as useful as knowing the symptoms that we discussed earlier when it comes to identifying social anxiety.

Introversion

To start with, let's look at what being an introvert truly means. In one of the later chapters, we will carefully consider a list of situations and settings that can be difficult for introverts, with or without social anxiety. For now, we'll stick to brass tacks. In practical terms, an introvert is a person who likes calm and relatively quiet environments and settings that aren't overly stimulating. While they might not scare the introvert, such situations can be mentally and emotionally draining for them, which is why introverts usually need a period of relaxation in solitude after a prolonged period of socializing. The more stimulating and intense that socialization is, the more of an effect it will have.

The concepts of introversion and extroversion in humans can be traced back to one of the most famous psychologists, Carl Jung, who introduced these terms in 1921. In its essence, this whole concept didn't primarily focus on sociability. Rather, Jung postulated that an introvert is simply someone who is more focused on and more attuned to their inner thoughts and feelings. It's a sort of inward focus characterized by things like frequent introspection and a focus on everything inside themselves. On the other hand, an extrovert is a person who focuses primarily or exclusively on the outside world.

Jung's theory later played an important party in other theories of personality, such as the "Big Five" theory, also known as the five-factor model. This is essentially a system of grouping personality traits, and it's still used today. Another well-known instance of the use of the introvert-extrovert scale is the Myers-Briggs Type Indicator or MBTI. This is a system and test that has been used for a while now to categorize people into pre-defined personality types, and an individual's introversion or extroversion plays an important role in that.

Over time, these terms have evolved, and various psychologists have given their contribution to evolving the definitions. Today, it's quite clear to us that introverts also tend to be less sociable than

extroverts, although, once again, they aren't necessarily socially anxious or even shy. When it comes to social or any other kinds of stimulation coming from the outside, extroverts tend not just to prefer but also need more of it. For instance, whereas an extrovert might need to go out to a party in the evening and engage with a lot of people to feel fulfilled, an introvert will usually prefer to sit at someone's home with two or three close friends and have a laid-back, quiet evening. All in all, introverts will focus on their internal feelings while extroverts focus on external stimulation.

All of this is best viewed as a spectrum between extroversion and introversion, meaning that there are few folks who are extremely introverted or extroverted. Most people are somewhere on the middle ground, but a lean toward one or the other is certainly apparent in most people. It's impossible to know the exact figure, but it is estimated that folks who can be defined as introverted account for some 25 to 40% of the population.

While social anxiety is, as we discussed, a disorder most likely caused by a combination of genetic and environmental factors, it's even less clear what causes introversion. On top of that, introversion is in no way considered a disorder. There are, of course, some proposed explanations. In general, introverts and extroverts are most likely born that way, but environmental factors can certainly play a part. After all, it's difficult to determine how exactly your personality forms. The important thing to understand is that introversion is perfectly normal and natural.

The key difference between social anxiety and introversion is that the former implies fear, while the latter is all about preference. While introversion is simply a way you live, social anxiety is something that keeps you from living. Furthermore, while the cause is broad, the inner workings of introversion and extroversion are well understood. A study published a few years ago in Frontiers in Human Neuroscience by Richard Depue and co-authors at the College of Human Ecology has given us more insight in this regard.

According to the researchers, introversion and extroversion have a lot to do with the way in which the reward system in an individual's brain works. It basically boils down to brain chemistry, notably dopamine. In the simplest terms, dopamine is a chemical that your brain releases to give you a rewarding sensation whenever you succeed at something or acquire a thing that you want. In the brains of extroverts, researchers say, there is a much higher and more stimulating response to dopamine. Because of this, extroverts are more motivated to seek out higher stimulation, which inevitably makes them more outgoing.

The Marks of an Introvert

You will learn more about how to differentiate between social anxiety and things like introversion as we proceed, but for now, let us look at some common signs of introversion. As you can probably gather by now, while there is a high correlation between introversion and slower social life, that doesn't mean that introverts can't be quite sociable. This is why performance in social situations is not always a reliable indicator. A much better indicator of introversion and extroversion is how an individual performs in solitude.

Solitude isn't really stimulating, which is why extroverts have a particularly difficult time dealing with it. If you find it easy or even preferable to spend time alone, that's a strong indicator of introversion. Do you find yourself enjoying a quiet evening at home with some hot chocolate and a book much more than a big party? Do you prefer small, quiet gatherings with a select few friends or relatives? These are signs that you are probably an introvert.

However, if you often find yourself incredibly bored, restless, and frustrated when you are alone, then you might be an extrovert. The thing is, however, that if you feel like this when alone but still struggle and feel incredibly uncomfortable in social situations, then this is a very good indicator that your problem is a social anxiety disorder.

This would be a clear case of fear over preference, as we mentioned earlier. You find yourself craving interaction and the stimulation that it brings, but you struggle with it, and that's when the problem goes beyond the matter of introversion and extroversion.

The reason why introverts will often feel that their energy has been drained after a while of socializing is not that they are necessarily unsociable, but because of their different response to stimulation. Consider how you feel after you go to a party or a large family gathering. Do you feel drained and worn out or recharged? Indeed, while social situations drain the introvert's energy, they recharge the extrovert.

Another common sign of introversion is deep and sophisticated introspection. If you tend to spend a lot of your waking hours in introspection, listening to your inner voice, daydreaming, and otherwise disregarding the world around you, then you are almost certainly an introvert. We already mentioned that introverts are characterized by a focus on their inner feelings, but that doesn't mean they're just more emotional. It has to do with the way introverts process all the input they receive from the outside world. The extrovert tends to perceive things externally while the introvert will internalize the information and process it through their intricate inner conversations and feelings.

All of this implies a high level of self-awareness, which might be the reason why introverts are more likely to be self-conscious and, in turn, socially anxious. Introverts tend to know themselves rather well, meaning that they are in touch with their emotions and understand their own motivations, thoughts, and ideas. If you're an introvert, this might seem like nothing special to you, but the truth is that a lot of people struggle with understanding what and why they feel most of the time or even why they do certain things. Introverts usually don't have that problem. In general, if you spend a lot of time soul-searching and trying to get to the bottom of your thoughts, you are likely introverted.

Introverts also can concentrate on things very closely, especially on one task at a time. If you prefer to maintain focus on one thing at a time instead of multitasking, that's a sign of introversion. Furthermore, when it comes to learning how to do a certain job or absorbing a new skill, introverts will usually prefer to learn through observation for a while before getting into the mix. This often entails learning from others by watching them perform. Extroverts tend to rely more on trial and error.

Introverts also like autonomy, particularly at work. It's not that introverts can't function as part of a team, but if they are given a choice, they tend to prefer jobs that provide them a dose of independence or even isolation. Not only would an introvert prefer such a job, but they tend to perform better on them as well.

Another clue you can look for is how others perceive you. Introverts are often mistaken for shy or anxious people, as you can imagine, and it happens primarily with strangers. Look at how you are seen by those who know you. If they can observe that you are usually quiet, somewhat reserved, and not eager to share the more intimate corners of your mind, you are probably an introvert.

Shyness

It can be argued that shyness has a lot more in common with social anxiety than introversion does. Of course, shyness is a concept that's a bit difficult to define. It's not a disorder or any sort of diagnosed illness and is much more informal and colloquial of an idea, so to speak. Different people might describe different traits as shyness. Just having one bad day where you don't feel particularly sociable can lead some folks to consider you as shy, even though you're usually not withdrawn at all.

Perhaps the most accurate definition of shyness would be to go back to the fear of judgment that happens with social anxiety as well. Some would describe shyness as a low-intensity or early-stage social anxiety. While they're not the same thing, social anxiety does indeed often look like shyness multiplied by ten. As such, shyness also often stems from simpler issues like low confidence, a poor self-image, and self-conscious attitudes.

However, the thing about shyness and introversion is that the latter can sometimes be forcibly turned into the former, so to speak. As natural and normal as introversion is, it's no secret that our society favors extroverts. It's certainly not some grand conspiracy to oppress introverts, of course, but that's just the way it is. Humans are social creatures, as we discussed, and our economy, society, and civilization itself all depend on the communication of all sorts. As such, we have naturally ended up with a society where extroverts will thrive.

The reason this is relevant is that regular, extroverted folks will sometimes misinterpret introversion for shyness or perceive it as anti-social, which can lead to introverts being ostracized and alienated. This is because they might feel that the way they are is undesirable and unwelcome, ingraining in them a belief that there is something fundamentally wrong with them. Of course, being alienated and shunned is devastating for any person's self-image, and, over time, that's how a healthy introvert might turn into a person suffering from SAD or a considerable level of shyness.

As Jonathan Rauch explained in a rather famous article in the Atlantic in the early 2000s, extroverts find it very difficult to understand the very idea of introversion. They can't relate to it, and this often leads to the misconceptions that we mentioned. Because of all this, introverts can even be labeled as arrogant, stuck-up, and much else.

Another core difference between introversion and shyness is that, unlike introversion, what we call shyness is often a response, not an inherent trait. Apart from just being shy, people can also get shy, in a situation that is. When you feel discomfort in a social situation, and that unpleasant feeling of being judged comes over you, you will usually end up being "shy."

As you can see, shyness can also be viewed and defined as a symptom of social anxiety disorder. But of course, it's not always like that, especially not in colloquial terms and everyday situations.

Regular people generally consider shyness to be a trait, and there is a fine balance that some people manage to create between their ability to socialize and their reserved nature. In fact, as you probably know, shyness is sometimes even seen as a virtue or at least as something likable or cute.

This is why shyness is perhaps the murkiest of all these concepts and the most difficult one to define. It's a word that we use so frequently that it's difficult to ascribe a scientific meaning and definition to it. As such, it's best to focus on the differences between introversion and social anxiety above all while considering shyness as a potential symptom of SAD.

One of the many attempts to define shyness was offered by experts in child behavior and personality psychology, Louis A. Schmidt and Arnold H. Buss. They have explained that sociability, as the opposite of shyness, represents a motivation to be with others. Shyness, on the other hand, refers to tension and discomfort among people, and usually certain behaviors in reaction to that discomfort.

Chapter Three: Anxiety vs. Worry vs. Fear

Anxiety has a lot in common with worry and especially with fear, but they're not all one and the same as far as psychology and psychiatry are concerned. This is the chapter where we will go into more detail on what anxiety, in general, really is and how it relates to some common psychological turmoil that we all experience at some point. In the previous chapter, we looked at personality traits that can resemble social anxiety while, in this one, we will focus on mental processes that every healthy human will experience at some point.

Indeed, there is hardly anything more natural and human than worrying or being fearful. Worrying means we care, and it can be very important, especially when it comes to our loved ones. Worrying can also give us signals and warnings as to potentially negative outcomes of certain choices or situations. Furthermore, fear is an indispensable part of our survival mechanism, and it has been as such for as long as we have walked the Earth.

The Shades and Structure of Anxiety

On top of what we have already discussed about the nature of social anxiety and its definition, it's also worth mentioning that social anxiety certainly exists on a spectrum and can be broken down into components. We already discussed early on how symptoms of social anxiety can be categorized, but there is also a three-part view of the structure of anxiety, which some experts will use.

Simply put, the three central components of your anxiety are the emotional, physiological, and cognitive components. The emotional component comprises the things you feel, such as fear or that sinking feeling of dread before a social engagement, for example. The physiological component just includes all those physical symptoms we discussed earlier. The cognitive component is where things get interesting, and this is also where worry falls in. This component is all about the thoughts you have, which are related to your anxiety.

Whenever you think about how you can't do something or about the many potential scenarios where you are embarrassed and humiliated, that's the cognitive component to your anxiety. As you can see, all of this will often entail worrying, and that's how worry comes into play when you're feeling anxious, especially before a social interaction takes place.

We also mentioned that social anxiety disorder exists on a certain spectrum. This is because, as we mentioned, a degree of anxiety happens naturally to most people at some point. The thing about normal anxiety, social or otherwise, is that it won't interfere in your daily life. This is because it happens rarely and because its symptoms are milder than with actual social anxiety disorder. When it occurs in this healthy, natural way, anxiety can even be good. In a social situation, that tiny amount of anxiety can make you more alert, focused, and lively, which some people will interpret positively.

As you start moving away from that side of the spectrum, you approach the levels of anxiety that can cause discomfort and make social situations undesirable for you. Further toward the other end, disorder territory begins when your anxiety hinders your performance in social and other situations and simply impairs you in anything from important tasks to daily life. In other words, it is natural sometimes to worry, but the moment you get to a situation where you would rather just stay home than face the music is when you should know that you probably have social anxiety.

There is also a certain gray area between natural anxiety and full-on impairment. This is where you might get symptoms of an anxiety disorder to a point where you experience regular discomfort. Nonetheless, you will probably find yourself limiting your social interactions and being less assertive, even though you are at least leaving your home. This level of social anxiety can be damaging for you in the long term as it can make you more reserved and unwilling to go the extra mile at work, for instance. Furthermore, being close to diagnosable social anxiety usually means the problem will get worse over time if you leave it unchecked.

Social anxiety can also come accompanied by panic attacks, which are sometimes similar but definitely not the same as anxiety attacks. Panic attacks are characterized by strong physical symptoms or at least a perception of such symptoms. Panic attacks are usually sudden and are triggered due to certain phobias, such as social phobia, in your case. One common physical symptom is an erratic heart rate and difficulties with breathing. Panic attacks won't kill you or give you an actual heart attack, but they can make you feel like it, which makes them scary.

There can be certain continuity between your anxiety and a panic attack because a panic attack can come as a sort of culmination of your anxiety. If you're being stressed out by a prolonged and highly unpleasant social situation, you might get to an overload where your mind just can't take it anymore and moves on to a whole new level of the fear response. Such a thing will never happen because of plain old worry. Panic attacks are very often indicative of an underlying anxiety problem and are always a sign of stress overload. All in all, even though it's a diagnosed mental disorder, social anxiety can sometimes be difficult to define, and it can involve a lot of gray areas.

Anxiety and Worry

Like fear, stress, or shyness, worry has something of a special relationship with anxiety while not being synonymous with it. As you well know, worry is an integral part of the symptoms of social anxiety, although it is sometimes confused with the disorder. It is natural and, in fact, characteristic of humans to engage in planning, as being able to make plans has been one of the decisive factors in getting us to where we are as a species.

Of course, to plan is to think ahead, consider different outcomes, and visualize scenarios. This will inevitably sometimes lead to worry, especially when the odds are objectively stacked against you, for instance. Worry is also normal if you're scheduled for an important job interview or any other social engagement that can directly impact the subsequent course of your life. Simply put, we worry often, and we often have good reasons to do so. Not only that, but worrying is sometimes the thing that keeps us going and helps us make the right decisions.

Still, that doesn't change the fact that worry also plays a prominent role in social anxiety. You now know how worry and anxiety relate to each other, but it's still possible to confuse the two since, as we mentioned, there's the natural worry that everyone experiences, and then there's the kind of worry that comes with outbreaks of anxiety.

One of the most important and immediately obvious differences between worry and anxiety, social or otherwise, is the physical nature of anxiety. Indeed, worry doesn't manifest physically and is instead limited to the confines of your mind. As such, if you have troubling thoughts about something that might happen, even if they get a bit uncontrollable, take note of whether you are experiencing the physical symptoms that we have discussed.

Furthermore, when social anxiety is involved, your worries will get extremely persistent, frequent, and often disproportionate or excessive. It's usually not good to compare yourself to others, but if you worry about going to the store with the same intensity as your friends or family members worry about a potentially life-changing job interview, then you have definitely moved past regular worry.

As we mentioned earlier, one of the key differences between anxiety and worry is that worry is all about what's going on in your thoughts while anxiety gets physical. Since both scenarios involve lots of thinking, though, it's also worth pointing out that worry is usually more specific than anxiety. What that means is that worry tends to focus on a very specific, real issue, whether it's small or big. You can be worried about being late to an appointment, but if you're also troubled by commuting or are obsessing over what might happen once you get to the appointment, then you are anxious. Anxiety is more general and can often get murky when it comes to its sources.

Another important difference is that worry can be productive, at least in the sense that it will often lead you to think of solutions to a problem. It's only natural that when you are worried about a specific issue, your mind will start to think of solutions to that problem. With anxiety, though, no solutions are found because the problem itself is not clear. Anxiety is unproductive and leaves you with no ideas as to how to get through a certain situation. It just gives you stress and fear.

Indeed, just focusing on your actual concerns and analyzing them as objectively as you can give you a better idea of whether you're anxious or just worrying. Next time you get to feeling worried or anxious, you should take a moment to consider what's bothering you. If you are concerned about going to work because you're up for a review, then you are worrying about a specific thing. If, on the other hand, you don't feel like going to work simply because you're afraid you might mess something up or get embarrassed in some way, this would be anxiety.

Worries are also easier to control than anxiety. This is in part because of what we just discussed about worry being more firmly rooted in reality. It's thus easier to get to the underlying problem and solve it, whereas anxiety is something you must struggle against on a much deeper level. Therefore, it is no surprise that worry also tends to be much more temporary than anxiety, which can linger, evolve, and get even more complex and unreasonable. In the simplest possible terms, worry is normal; anxiety is not.

Anxiety and Fear

The relationship between fear and anxiety is very similar to that of anxiety and worry. Just like worry, fear is natural, normal, and even helpful, so it differs from anxiety even though it is one of its common symptoms. Fear is even more specific and focused than worry. Whereas your anxiety is diffuse, your fear response is usually brought on by something very real and immediate – something that's easily identified. Unlike with the general feeling of dread that torments you in seemingly normal social situations, your fear is what alerts you to danger, lets you know when to act, and would keep you alive in the wilderness.

Fear can have many of the same symptoms as anxiety, particularly physical symptoms. It can make you sweat or tremble, and it can hike up your heart rate, but the difference is that the threat is real, while, with anxiety, it is imagined or blown completely out of proportion in your mind. Both fear and anxiety can cause each other or make each other worse as well.

Once again, unlike anxiety, fear is something that isn't chronic, and it doesn't have the potential to ruin your life. It will come and go, and as unpleasant as it might be, it will go away when it's no longer needed or justified. In social situations, fear can be justified in many instances, especially when strangers are involved. It's natural to respond with at least a small amount of fear if you're approached by someone in a dark alleyway. Your mind is analyzing the setting, and it seems quite a few real possibilities of danger, so it warns you about that. On the other hand, if you react to interaction in the same way when you are going to the bank, for instance, then you most likely have social anxiety instead of any fear of a real threat.

In a way, fear is anxiety, and anxiety is fear. This is because they are so similar in nature, while only their root cause is different. It is also that difference in causes that make anxiety a persistent, nagging feeling while fear is very temporary. Anxiety persists because it is caused by such vague and abstract threats that only exist in the projected and imagined scenario that has emerged in your mind. It's difficult to solve a problem that you can't really see or even describe to someone else, so anxiety remains, and it follows you around.

After a while, you can get to a point where your anxiety has caused enough tangible damage to your life for you to start fearing the anxiety itself. And why wouldn't you? If it has damaged your career, caused you embarrassment, and devastated your social life, your social anxiety is a threat to you – a very real and objective one at that. It is certainly a strange blend of real and abstract since the anxiety itself is just in your mind, but it's a very real vicious cycle that many sufferers of SAD end up in.

As you can see, fear, worry, and shyness all have connections and relationships with social anxiety disorder, and why they are not synonymous, they play prominent parts. All three of these things can occur naturally, but when social anxiety is at play, all three can become persistent and exhausting. As you will learn through this book, this whole problem can be approached from both ends. Namely, some folks have successfully beaten their social anxiety disorders by attacking their fears and worries head-on. On the other hand, some prefer to address the disorder through therapy and other such approaches that go straight to the disease.

In either case, the result will be the same if you are successful. The chronic and irrational aspect of these feelings is what you must remove from your life. You will still get to feel fear and worry, of course, and you might even get shy at times, but you will no longer be at the whim of your unpredictable and ever-present anxiety. In a way, the goal is not just to interact and socialize like a regular person, but also to fear and to worry like a regular, healthy person.

Chapter Four: Ten Common Fears Introverts Have

As we already discussed, introversion is something that people often confuse with social anxiety. Regardless, social anxiety is indeed often part of an introvert's life, and so the two do correlate. Because of this, we can understand social anxiety better if we also get a better understanding of the introverted mind. In this chapter, we will go over some of the situations and experiences that introverts might fear or prefer to avoid, especially if they have social anxiety. This should help you get an even better understanding of the differences between anxiety and introversion but also how they can work together at times.

This list should also help you categorize some of your experiences and reactions to certain situations. You will thus be better equipped to identify whether you're struggling with anxiety or are just introverted. For each of these situations or environments, we will also consider how a socially anxious individual might react to them as opposed to someone who is merely an introvert.

Small Talk

Like most things we'll discuss in this chapter, small talk is something that comes completely naturally to folks who have no problems with social interaction. It's something that's meant to pass the time, allow us to analyze the other person, or just entertain us. Introverts are usually not fans of small talk and meaningless chit-chat, in general, but that's not always because they fear it.

When social anxiety is at play, however, small talk becomes scary because, instead of being a frivolous pastime, it provides ample opportunity to feel judged and scrutinized. A socially anxious person will spend every second of that small talk obsessing over how they look or sound and constantly fretting over what the other person might be thinking about them. Even when it's obvious that the conversational partner is not judgmental or noticing anything strange about us, the mind that's stricken with social anxiety will be clouded by irrational fear.

In fact, small talk might be one of the worst and most stressful forms of conversation that a socially anxious person might get into. When a conversation is deep, thoughtful, meaningful, and, most importantly, interesting, it will captivate the mind more easily and direct the thoughts away from that anxious path. You should consider the way you think and act during small talk to see where you fall on the spectrum.

Crowds

This one is something of a no-brainer, but crowds are something that's very difficult for introverts to deal with. Introverts will prefer calmer, quieter settings such as resting at home or sitting around with a select group of close friends. As such, introverts tend to avoid crowds simply because they don't get anything out of the experience. When they are also socially anxious, though, they will see crowds as a scary prospect, not just a hassle.

The fear will be exacerbated if the socially anxious introvert is alone. Think about a scenario such as being alone in a bar or at a party and how it would make you feel or how it has made you feel if you've ever experienced it. Crowded places have a way of making some people feel even more alone than usual, especially if they are introverted. Your social anxiety might also make you feel like everyone is judging you, and this feeling can make people seem inaccessible. When feeling alone or left out in such a setting, the normal course of action is to start up a conversation with someone, but social anxiety makes that incredibly difficult. The sight of others engaging in conversations so effortlessly and having great fun can also make matters worse.

Healthy introverts will sincerely and wholeheartedly prefer to sit at home by the fireplace and read a book, with that being the reason they don't go to parties. Socially anxious folks, on the other hand, will not go because of their fears, even though they might yearn for the experience.

Meeting New People

As we just mentioned, social anxiety makes it incredibly difficult to approach people and start conversations, which makes meeting new people a chore. The thing about introverts, even socially anxious ones, is that they might already have a couple of close friends, especially if they are childhood friends, and still struggle to meet new people. Because of this, just because you have some friends doesn't mean that you're not socially anxious or introverted.

Meeting new people is difficult for socially anxious people both as a prospect and as a reality when it happens. This means that SAD will make you want to avoid situations where you know you might get to meet someone new. You might feel deep down like you have a desire to meet new people, but your fear of judgment and embarrassment will often be stronger than that desire.

Something that healthy introverts should have no problem with is being approached by a stranger and engaging in conversation with them. When you have social anxiety, interaction is stressful even when the other person initiates contact and breaks the ice. You might begin feeling the symptoms and then start to worry about the person noticing there's something wrong with you, and things can spiral out of control in no time.

Giving a Speech

Giving a speech is a nightmare for many people, and it can be stressful even for extroverts, depending on the situation and how important the speech is. Introverts don't enjoy being the center of attention at gatherings, and they certainly prefer to stick to the sidelines while others do the public speaking. For socially anxious folks, on the other hand, giving a speech is a scenario that probably most closely resembles hell.

It's unfortunate that a lot of regular people don't really have much understanding of introverts, much less those with social anxiety. In settings like weddings or other familial gatherings, introverts are sometimes pushed by others into situations where they must speak. The thing is, though, that most people aren't gifted speakers, and they will generally try to avoid that role by default, so it doesn't necessarily imply that social anxiety is at play.

Regular folks will be able to improvise, though, and they won't find the possibility of embarrassment as terrifying as socially anxious people will. As such, if you're merely reluctant but still don't start feeling nauseous, dizzy, or panicked, it's just your introversion.

Public Transport and Elevators

Public transport is a double-edged sword when it comes to social anxiety. It's difficult to determine which is worse: when the train or bus is absolutely packed with strangers or when there's just you and one or two other people, increasing the chances of you drawing their attention.

Public transportation can get really crowded, so it's only natural to be annoyed when your personal space is being invaded and when you're physically uncomfortable. Regular introverts will deal with these conditions by shutting the world off via headphones and music or by reading a book. Social anxiety can make even that difficult, though, as the feeling of being watched or judged can sometimes be intense enough to break through your attempts at distraction.

Elevators are another problem area when you have social anxiety. The upside is that the elevator ride is usually over very quickly, but the confined space of the elevator can make for some rather awkward moments when you find yourselves in there with only one other person. Again, a regular introvert will be able to just keep to themselves for a few seconds and go about their business; however, with social anxiety, that short elevator ride can be incredibly stressful and mentally exhausting.

Open-Plan Offices

Introverts tend to feel the most comfortable on jobs where they get to work alone for extended periods or are at least given an office of their own where they can retreat. Open-plan offices are severely restricting when it comes to privacy, so this can be a very exhausting environment for an introvert, especially when there's also social anxiety to contend with.

However, the human brain's ability to adapt to a routine is quite impressive! If a routine is solid and predictable enough, even a socially anxious person can get used to an environment such as this. If there are always the same people around, with the same conditions and the same sort of work and interaction, you might get used to it after a while and function normally while at work. As soon as you find

yourself in a new situation, or there is a sudden change; however, your anxiety might kick right back in.

Because of this, you shouldn't be confused if you find yourself talking to your coworkers and working with them without a problem, but then fail to interact with people at a bar or some other such place. What's more, introverts can get incredibly communicative and sociable once they get used to a circle of people, to a point where, when observed from the side, they seem extroverted.

Phone Calls

Outbreaks of social anxiety are not exclusive to face-to-face interactions. Making phone calls is something that most introverts don't enjoy, except when it's to someone they are completely comfortable with. Social anxiety makes phone calls difficult on a whole new level, though, especially when the call is important or involves a stranger.

Regular folks can go on and on over the phone while doing other things around the house or even while working. With social anxiety, though, your mind will be unable to focus on anything other than the phone call, and you will either sit frozen in place or pace around the room nervously the entire time. Physical symptoms of anxiety and all the discomfort that they bring might then ensue. You might start having shortness of breath, and your voice might begin to shake.

As usual, when those symptoms happen, there will be a high possibility of further fears over the other person noticing there's something wrong, further worsening the anxiety. For socially anxious folks, the only advantage of phone calls is that they can usually be promptly cut off. Other than that, for many sufferers of SAD, phone calls are just as stressful as personal interactions. Furthermore, telephonophobia is a phobia that exists, and it's exactly what you would imagine. The fear of making phone calls and the fear of social interaction can essentially make phone calls the scariest form of interaction for some introverts.

Surprises

Surprises - particularly those that entail social situations and interactions - are a great enemy of many introverts, especially socially anxious ones. Things that break routines and cause upsets that can lead to unexpected situations and unexpected people can be dreadful. These surprises can entail big changes in the work environment, for instance, in which case they are there to stay, but they can also come in the form of more trivial situations like surprise parties.

As you can imagine, a sudden and unexpected social situation is not something that introverts are known to enjoy, much less when they struggle with social anxiety. If you've ever been thrown a surprise party or experienced something similar, you should know how it made you feel. Extroverts would immediately know how to act, and they would probably be happy to receive such attention, but introversion and social anxiety can lead to a panicked response.

Of course, the main problem with these situations is in the very center of attention for everyone in the room. As usual, that kind of spotlight is a socially anxious person's greatest fear. Still, surprise parties might have a different effect in some instances. For some people, social anxiety is at its worst when a social situation is anticipated, and when they have plenty of time to obsess over it and think of a million negative scenarios. A surprise party might occupy your mind immediately and not give you any time to think, which can be a good thing with social anxiety.

Scrutiny

Any kind of scrutiny can be difficult for folks with social anxiety, especially in public. Therefore, things like job interviews are so difficult for introverted folks. It's not just a question of fearing the scrutiny itself, either. You might end up being afraid of showing symptoms of your anxiety while being scrutinized, even if you're confident in your knowledge, skill, or competence.

For instance, people with social anxiety are often afraid to write in front of others. They are afraid that their hand will start to shake, and that the other person will notice it. It's one of those situations where anxiety and the fear of that anxiety feed into each other and form a stressful cycle. There are countless other similar examples, some of which you have likely experienced at some point. Therefore, socially anxious people can fail where they shouldn't.

As an example, they can study for a long time and be well-prepared for a test, but the unbearable discomfort of scrutiny can still make them fail the test. It's why they end up not getting jobs that they are qualified for or a promotion that they more than deserve. It's unfair, and it amounts to nothing short of being robbed of all the good things in life.

Embarrassment

Last (but not least), embarrassment, particularly in public, is something that's very difficult to deal with for introverts - let alone socially anxious ones! As mentioned before, in most cases of social anxiety disorder, the fear of embarrassment is the very core of the condition.

Certainly, everybody can get embarrassed or humiliated, but the difference between regular folks and those with social anxiety is that the former doesn't spend a lot of time thinking about the prospect of embarrassment, whereas the latter does. The potential to get embarrassed is usually the first thing to pop into the mind of a socially anxious person when they consider a possible social situation they might get into. The fear is the most decisive factor that makes you avoid social situations or gives you second thoughts.

People who are only introverted might not handle embarrassment well, but they won't have the same obsession with that risk prior to the situation. Furthermore, social anxiety can make you feel embarrassed even though there really isn't anything to be embarrassed about. This is especially true when there's low self-esteem at play, as it can make you much more likely to feel embarrassed or humiliated.

That's how and why those situations and settings affect introverts or introverts with social anxiety. It's another list that can function as a checklist of symptoms and signs for you to use to get better acquainted with your case.

Chapter Five: How Psychological Triggers Work

Of course, social anxiety doesn't just come up out of nowhere. We already mentioned a thing or two about the cause of the disorder itself, but now we will look at what goes on in your brain when any individual anxiety attack occurs. This chapter is all about understanding your own mind better in addition to getting to know more about what social anxiety is and how it works.

We also listed several potentially triggering situations and how introverts and socially anxious folks might react to them. These situations can be viewed as psychological triggers that lead to outbursts of anxiety, but why and how does that happen? What is it that your mind is doing wrong, and how can you begin to fix it? The truth is that your mind and instincts are doing what they were designed to do, but they are doing it at the wrong time and under the wrong circumstances.

Something else we'll look at is the concept of psychological triggers in relation to things like post-traumatic stress. This can be another source of social and any other kind of anxiety, so it's another important topic to discuss in that it will help you understand anxiety even better.

The Inner-Workings of Anxiety

As we mentioned, your anxiety is a fear response that becomes chronic and revolves around mostly abstract objects of fear. You can view your anxiety as a malfunction of your natural survival mechanisms that are otherwise useful and necessary. It's as if you had an important and sophisticated alarm system in your home, which, unfortunately, goes off all the time, ringing and blaring for no good reason at all, driving you nuts.

When it works like it's meant to, your flight-or-fight response is indeed supposed to stress you out, but that's just for a little while and because it's meant to give you a temporary boost to help you escape or fight the threat. This is something that virtually all animals have in some form of another. You might be inclined to think that the malfunctions of this system, like anxiety, are uniquely human, but that's not true. Animals can be traumatized, for instance, causing them to remember the trauma and experience severe anxiety whenever they are reminded of it.

Furthermore, take the example of a dog that was too sheltered and not properly exposed to the world like a puppy. Such dogs will often grow up to be anxious and afraid in all unfamiliar environments and situations. We're not much different at all with both examples. Our anxieties, social or otherwise, can often be tied to past trauma that's brought back every time the internalized stressful memory gets triggered, as we'll discuss in a bit more detail soon. On top of that, the more we isolate ourselves from the world, the worse our insecurities and anxieties will get. Children who have trouble socializing or are overly sheltered, for instance, will often develop social anxiety or a range of other behavioral issues. Of course, as you know by now, these things are only some of the potential causes of anxiety. The difficulty of identifying the real, underlying cause is really one of the characteristics of anxiety, to begin with.

We do, however, have a rather detailed understanding of the inner workings of anxiety and of the process involved. As usual, your brain acts first, and then the body follows. Like most things, anxiety and fear have specific parts of the brain that are responsible for regulating them. We know this thanks to brain imaging technology and our understanding of neurochemicals and what they do. To put things simply, the two parts of your brain that are usually at the epicenter of almost all anxiety disorders are the amygdala and the hippocampus.

These parts of your brain have roles that are very important and extend well beyond just your simple fear responses. Your amygdala, located deep in your brain, is like an intersection or hub for communications. The parts of your brain that register and process sensory signals and the parts that make sense of those signals use the amygdala to communicate with each other. Being at such a junction, the amygdala is in the position to detect those signals that can be interpreted as threatening.

As such, the amygdala can put your brain on alert and lead to a fear response when needed. Your amygdala can also store memories that are emotional in nature, such as attachments or associations between certain things you have experienced. Therefore, the amygdala is believed to play a role in all sorts of fear-related things, including anxiety disorders and phobias.

On the other hand, the hippocampus deals specifically with memorizing and internalizing events and experiences where you were threatened or felt as such. The role of the hippocampus in things like flashbacks, trauma, post-traumatic stress, and similar problems is still being studied. Researchers have hitherto managed to confirm that the hippocampus in people who were exposed to abuse as children or have participated in a war is smaller. It's not the case 100% of the time, but there is a strong correlation, as outlined by the National Institute of Mental Health.

Without going into too much scientific detail, something else you should keep in mind is the role of neurochemicals in the process behind your anxiety. When your mind and body enter their flight-or-fight mode, your brain will ramp up the production of organic chemicals like norepinephrine and hormones like cortisol. Cortisol is an especially famous one, and it is commonly referred to as the stress hormone.

Both substances are completely natural and normal, as their role is to give you important boosts in potentially life-threatening situations. Their purpose is to make you alert, quick, and overall stimulated. This is what leads to all those physiological symptoms that we have discussed, like a heightened heart rate and erratic breathing. In this state, your body and mind will disregard or outright shut down many other processes so that they can both focus on one simple task, which is to keep you alive.

In your case, your mind has become convinced that it is the threat of humiliation and embarrassment that is life-threatening, so it acts accordingly. Both your mind and body are doing what they are supposed to do, but they are doing it for the wrong reason, and that's the core of the problem. That is how anxiety emerges and how it works. The cause is one thing, but there are also triggers, such as those we have discussed in the previous chapter. There are also triggers that can be more personal and internalized, as opposed to completely external.

Psychological Triggers

Psychological triggers are something that can often be the thing that sets an individual's anxiety in motion. The triggers themselves usually have an underlying cause, such as trauma, so they can't really be the cause of social anxiety in their own right. They can, however, provide the spark that provokes an anxious response, which, in turn, can lead to an exacerbated anxiety brought on by the fear of these triggers.

A psychological trigger can come in many forms, including smells, sights, sounds, or other things that can trigger a traumatic response. Therefore, triggers are usually associated with things like post-traumatic stress disorder, or PTSD. These triggers are reminders, and they bring to the surface and internalized memory and fear of a trauma that has transpired in the past. Such reminders of traumatic experiences usually lead to anxiety, panic attacks, or at least an intense sense of dread. In more extreme cases, the sufferer can also experience flashbacks.

These vivid outbursts of involuntary and accurate remembering can feel like the person is reliving the traumatic event all over again. Flashbacks can lead to a complete albeit temporary dissociation from the environment and from the current reality. People who experience flashbacks can "lose" time or become utterly disoriented for a while. As such, the anxiety can be just one of the symptoms, and when such responses occur in social situations, traumatized people can be mistaken for just being socially anxious when, in fact, the problem is even deeper.

These triggers can include the simplest, most innocuous of things, if these things can - in some way - bring up past trauma. Sometimes, the response can come about as a result of too much stress as well, in which case the trigger isn't even external. As you can probably imagine, a simple example of one of these triggers can be a smell that the sufferer has smelled during the traumatic event. A war veteran, for instance, can be triggered by the smell of gunpowder. There can really be a million different triggers in a million different personal stories of trauma.

We still don't know everything about how and why our minds internalize and respond to these triggers the way they do. Some believe that it once again all goes back to our fight or flight response in situations perceived to be threatening. The most bewildering thing about trauma, triggers, and all these other things is that different people can be affected differently by the same things. Not everyone who was abused as a child will carry the trauma, some people come back from war mostly unchanged, and some, even though they are traumatized, won't necessarily be triggered and anxious.

We mentioned earlier that your mind and body would disregard various processes that aren't essential for survival when a flight-or-fight situation arises. One of these processes is the formation of your short-term memories. Herein lays one of the theories about how psychological triggers work. Namely, it's possible that your brain can take an ongoing traumatic experience and store it in the wrong file cabinet, so to speak.

Instead of putting this event into the category of past events that become regular memories, like the time you went to the beach, your brain can categorize the event as an ongoing threat. As such, every reminder (trigger) will bring that experience back to the surface, even years down the road, and your brain will be tricked into thinking that it's happening again. Your mind and body will then enter flight-or-fight mode again, and you will shut down and become unable to control your anxiety or outright panic.

You can imagine how this plays out in the context of social anxiety. If a past trauma revolves around public humiliation, bullying, or something similar, it's not difficult to see how the most public, social situations could act as a trigger.

Something else that experts have been looking at is the sensory component in triggers. Things like sights, sounds, smells, and tastes are some of the strongest building blocks for memories. As such, the most intense and vivid memories are often those that include sensory stimuli, especially smell and taste. Such memories are also the easiest to remember, so a trigger that involves these senses can be incredibly powerful.

If you've ever experienced the onset of memories that can happen when you taste a certain dish or smell something, then you have seen this mechanism at work. Your brain is simply wired to take special note of that sensory information, and that comes into play during regular and traumatic events alike.

Another thing about these sensory triggers is that they can work alone, regardless of context. You can find yourself in a situation that's completely different than the one where the traumatic event took place, but if you sense the triggering smell, for instance, it will be enough to cause a reaction.

As such, these sensory triggers can also be rather *stealthy*. You might get anxious or otherwise emotional even before you realize what's happening and why, and you might not even notice the smell or connect it to what you are feeling. Your brain notices these things, though, and unless you know how to listen, it can be difficult to get to the root of the problem.

What's particularly tricky about all this is that such triggers can lead to episodes that can be misinterpreted as social anxiety. For instance, a sensory trigger of past trauma can occur while you are in a social situation, leading to an outbreak of anxiety or a panic attack even if the trauma has nothing to do with social situations. Interacting with people in such a state is going to be difficult, of course, so it might come across as social anxiety.

The ways in which you can deal with these triggers are as variable as the triggers and their causes. If your triggers indeed have to do with socializing or if you harbor past traumas associated with social situations, then the methods we will discuss throughout the rest of this book can help you. However, as we just discussed, psychological triggers can be tied to many experiences that don't have to do with socializing. In those cases, it might be a good idea to seek professional help, especially if you are having difficulties identifying the source of these triggers in the first place.

You should especially talk to a professional if you have reason to believe that you might be suffering from PTSD; it is very serious condition that can lead to a whole range of complications, including a complete breakdown - or even death. Healing from PTSD can be a long and painful journey that will require not just the help of professionals, but also that of your loved ones.

That's what psychological triggers are and how they work, particularly in the context of trauma, stress, and anxiety. It's not something that anybody should have to live with, and it's certainly not a problem that should be avoided or catered to. If certain things trigger anxious or panic reactions from you, then you should address the problem instead of just avoiding the trigger. Of course, if the reactions are extreme, then full and abrupt exposure is not the way to go, but gradual exposure and conditioning will usually be parts of the treatment in such cases.

Chapter Six: Negative Thoughts – Identify and Break Out of Them

As you have undoubtedly realized by now, social anxiety is largely based on a cycle of negative thoughts that are usually irrational and do little more than getting your mind racing and your thoughts clouded. Although some of the worries that trouble folks with SAD are universal, these negative thoughts usually vary from one individual to the next. An important step toward beating your social anxiety will be to identify your negative thoughts and your mental patterns that lead to a downward spiral of anxiety. You will then have to learn how to break free from these thoughts and, better yet, replace them with positive ones.

We've already briefly mentioned the importance of thinking positively, but, in this chapter, we will go into more detail on how exactly you can categorize the contents of your mind and clean up troubling thoughts. Rewiring your brain in this way can entail a lot of work, and it tends to be more difficult than many people anticipate, but every person who isn't severely mentally ill has the capacity to put a leash on their thoughts and get back in the driver's seat, *and you do, too.*

Understanding and Identifying Negative Thought Patterns

Negative thoughts can be strangely appealing to a mind that's used to them. What's more, when you indulge in certain negative thoughts for a while, they can easily snowball, getting worse over time. Because our brains naturally respond to patterns, they sometimes have a strange way of getting tangled up in patterns of negative thinking. This is how your thoughts can spiral uncontrollably and lead to a complete breakdown of reason during an anxious episode.

You may become so accustomed to these thoughts that you arrive at a place where you don't even know that the thoughts you are having are negative and detrimental for you. Therefore, the first step is to learn how to *identify negative thoughts and find the patterns in your thinking* that need to be dealt with.

After a while of living with low self-esteem and constantly delving into negative thinking, you will likely also develop automatic negative thoughts. These are thoughts that more closely resemble a sort of self-deprecating reflex that occurs every time you think of a potential social situation. For instance, if, upon being invited to go to a party, the first thing that come to mind is that you will be made fun of or that you will just embarrass yourself, then you are trapped in a cycle of automatic negative thoughts. This is usually what comes of prolonged social anxiety that's left unchecked.

This sort of thinking can quickly become routine as your mind loves nothing more than to recognize patterns and get comfortable in a routine. The degree to which your thoughts can influence and shape your feelings and life, in general, is underestimated. That goes for both conscious thoughts and those that are more involuntary and automatic.

Being that they are so deeply ingrained and involuntary, your automatic thoughts can be rather elusive, so identifying them might take some work. One of the ways to do this is to write down as many of your thoughts as you can - especially those that have to do with your self-image and opinion of yourself. The contents of our minds tend to look a whole lot different when we put them down on paper; on paper, we can take a more objective look and inspect that information with more impartiality.

You should try and do this on the fly, writing the thoughts down precisely when they happen instead of sitting down in the afternoon and trying to remember the thoughts. You can use your phone or a small notebook for this purpose and just write down what comes to mind in simple notes. As you write, you are likely to get even more thoughts going in your head, and because you will be writing, all of them will appear clearer. Don't focus too much on judging these thoughts or thinking about them. It's usually even better if you simply write them down and then look at the notes later.

You might be surprised to learn just how much negativity there is in your thoughts and how quickly you are to indulge them. With social anxiety, your mind will get flooded by negative thoughts in normal social situations, not just situations where you get embarrassed or experience some sort of failure. This habit of quickly jumping into a whirl of negativity is referred to as "negativity bias" by many neuroscientists and psychologists.

And that's precisely what it is – you simply have a bias toward the negative side of things, and that's what needs changing or at least controlling. The thing about your negativity bias is that it's natural to a degree, once again going back to survival instincts from our cave-dwelling days. The assumption of the worst-case scenario was useful and lifesaving for our ancestors in the wild, but these days, it can be a nuisance. Of course, the real problems begin when the negativity bias goes into the extreme.

This whole process was described in detail by Rick Hanson, a neuroscientist, and author of Buddha's Brain. In this book, Hanson describes the proclivity of your mind to focus on the negative while disregarding the positive experiences. When you have even more negative experiences than the regular person, which is all but guaranteed with social anxiety, your brain will eventually get outright obsessive with its focus on the negative side of everything.

Common Negative Thinking Patterns

The patterns and cycles of intensely negative thinking can vary a lot from one person to the next, but some patterns are universal and are experienced by most anxious people at some point. You are likely to identify with most if not all of these if you have social anxiety. Even without anxiety, though, many people can still fall into these patterns at least for a short while at some point in their lives.

One example of a negative thinking pattern is what can be referred to as cynical hostility. This one is especially characteristic of social anxiety and even plain introversion. As you might have gathered from the term itself, this is an attitude of deep distrust and hostility, whether internal or expressed, toward other people. This tends to happen when a person spends enough time with a disdain for social interaction or has accumulated enough negative experiences.

Of course, the troublesome part is that these negative experiences could have transpired because of the person's social anxiety. This means that the negative experience might not have been the fault of other people or, in some cases, even real. Social anxiety can certainly make you anxious and turn an interaction into an unpleasant memory even if nothing particularly problematic happens. Just the feeling of anxiety can be enough to create a strong distaste for people, even when the interaction transpires objectively well.

Cynical hostility will make you see the worst in people and always assume that they are doing or planning to do something against you. It is characteristic of hostile cynics to assume that the other person is trying to cheat or lie in some way, and the assumption that the cynic is being judged is also omnipresent. In severe cases, folks can start to project this even on their loved ones and the people they've been close with for years.

This can ruin relationships and lead to all sorts of upheaval and emotional turmoil in your life. Not to mention, some research suggests that there is a correlation between cynical hostility and heart problems later in life. Perhaps the weight of constantly keeping your guard up and always worrying about who is out to get you can wear you out after a couple of decades.

Negative rumination is another big one, especially when you consider the obsessiveness of anxiety. Negative rumination is the psychological and mental equivalent of a hamster wheel or a car stuck in the mud. It exerts a lot of energy and wears you out, but it ultimately gets you nowhere. This pattern is introspection and self-reflection taken to the extreme, particularly the negative extreme.

It occurs when you routinely get fixated on the negative or perceived negative aspects of yourself, reflecting on them to excessive lengths and very frequently, repeatedly. It's also possible to negatively ruminate outward as well, such as when you obsess over negative scenarios and outcomes of in situations that haven't even happened. The same can apply for past events that have left you feeling embarrassed. Negative rumination is when you can't stop thinking about what you did wrong or what you could have done better, to the point of driving yourself almost crazy.

This mental pitfall can exacerbate your anxiety and lead to a lot of other problems like depression, low self-esteem, mood swings, et cetera. Soon enough, you might catch yourself excessively thinking about the very fact that you are feeling anxious and low, which can become an obsession in and of itself.

Next up, you have your plain old overthinking. Overthinking can also take the form of perfectionism, and it usually leads to indecisiveness, reluctance, fear, and anxiety. At the core of the issue lies the false notion that it's possible to avoid all mistakes and remove all risk from the equation, which is, of course, impossible. It is very likely that you are familiar with this thinking pattern.

Whereas regular folks can just seamlessly get into social situations and interact without even thinking about it, people with social anxiety tend to obsess over doing everything right before they get on with it. This just builds up the anxiety and increases your reluctance, often ending with you prefer just to walk away.

These are just some of the negative thinking patterns that you might be familiar with. Perhaps you're so used to them that this is the first time you hear that this sort of thinking is bad for you. Indeed, these mental pitfalls can feel deceptively natural when you have anxiety, but they are really excessing that are making things way more difficult than they should be.

Shifting Your Mindset

Once you have acquainted yourself with the way your mind works and identifies the problematic thoughts that you need to move past, your next step is to shift your thinking and your whole mindset toward the positive. This isn't just about thinking a happy thought when you feel low. The ultimate goal is to permanently change your outlook and shift your mindset in the long term.

Take the patterns we have just discussed, for instance. There are methods you can start implementing right away, which can really alter your outlook and make you see the world in a new light. If you have identified yourself with cynical hostility, you should try to take a mental note of when you are thinking those thoughts and try to find alternatives. In a way, you should try and catch yourself in that pattern and make a conscious effort to replace the thought.

The simplest example is when people give you a compliment. A cynically hostile person will almost always assume there is an ulterior motive at play and that the other person is just flattering them because they want something. Of course, that's usually not the case, and a compliment tends to be just that – a compliment. Try and adopt the same mindset for all sorts of other behaviors that you have interpreted negatively in the past.

Put your judgment and negative assumptions on a leash, and don't let them be the automatic, first response. You can do this by focusing on evidence or the lack thereof. When you get to thinking that the other person is plotting or judging you, ask yourself if you have even a shred of evidence to support that assumption. The chances are good that you will have none. Simply put, you should try and apply the age-old principle of presumed innocence.

Negative rumination is even easier to beat. Since it is a cycle of repetition, all you must do is break that cycle as soon as you notice it's arising. Don't limit yourself just to the thoughts that have to do with your social anxiety or introversion. Whenever you catch yourself ruminating, no matter what it might be about, you should break the cycle. All you must do is give your mind someone else to toy with – ideally something productive and constructive. Creative hobbies are an excellent alternative to sitting and obsessing over thoughts that give you nothing but suffering. It doesn't matter what creative endeavor it is or how unskilled you are; the point is to get your mind busy.

You can also just go walk your dog or go to the store and stock up on groceries or engage in several other menial activities to keep your thoughts at bay. The two things that you should not do, however, are drinking alcohol and overeating just to drown out your mind. These are bad solutions that will almost always do more harm than good.

As for overthinking, the cliché that you should just do it certainly holds true. That's not to say that you shouldn't think about your actions at all, far from it, but the time you spend thinking should be reduced. You should especially cut down on that time when it comes to taking harmless action like talking to people. It's natural to spend some time thinking before you make big life decisions, of course, but thinking of a million (negative) scenarios and outcomes before starting a conversation with a stranger at the park serves virtually no purpose. Besides, the one thing you need to realize and fully internalize is that it's okay to mess up and that even if you get embarrassed, the consequences will be objectively harmless.

What we're talking about is something along the lines of the "notice-shift-rewire" approach. This is a pretty simple strategy to help you rewire your brain and shift its focus toward the positive side of things. This is a well-developed and tested strategy that has been in the works for a long time and has evolved for years.

Basically, the first step is all about noticing that negativity bias in your mind. As we have discussed, it's all about catching yourself in the act. It will probably take some practice to reach this level of awareness, but it's certainly doable. Make sure you use the tips we discussed, such as writing down your thoughts, at least at first.

The "shift" step includes all those changes in thinking that we've mentioned. In general, though, if you are trying to escape from overall negativity as quickly as possible, one recommended approach is to use gratitude. Indeed, just thinking about at least one thing you're grateful for in your life can ground you now and put your obsessive, negative thoughts into a more manageable perspective. You must remember that there is always something. Even if you're bankrupt, you might still have your health. And if you're ill, you probably have parents. If you look hard enough, there will always be something.

The last step that has to do with "rewiring" is the key and the end goal of the whole process. That's what you will essentially be doing – rewiring your brain and changing its habits. All the efforts we have just discussed can be taken up on the fly and integrated into your daily routine. All you must do is remember to bring yourself to the present, be more mindful of your thoughts, and get to work replacing the unwanted ones to get rid of this dead weight. The exercise we will discuss in the next chapter can also be helpful in that regard.

Chapter Seven: How Mindfulness Can Help with Social Anxiety

When it comes to the cognitive side of beating your social anxiety, mindfulness can be an indispensable tool. After all, mindfulness itself is all about cognition and the way you think. In the simplest terms, mindfulness implies being truly present in and engaged with the moment you find yourself in. It is a mental exercise to help you streamline your thoughts, quiet the mental noise, and ultimately put your mind at ease. It's essentially a meditative exercise, but don't let that dissuade you, as it's not a complicated or particularly advanced exercise and can be undertaken by laypersons without a problem.

The value of mindfulness in combating social anxiety is in that it's meant to clear your mind and streamline your thoughts, blocking out the anxiety-inducing mental noise that causes your problem. While you can fight on other fronts to boost your confidence and change your outlook from negative to positive, for instance, mindfulness can be an additional tool to help you rein your mind in for further maintenance. In this chapter, we will take a detailed look at what mindfulness really is and how you can use it to fight social anxiety.

What Is Mindfulness?

In practical terms, mindfulness is a process that is meditative in nature and focuses on shifting your attention in a certain way. That way is toward each present moment that you find yourself in, without worry about the future scenarios or dwelling on past ones. The objective is to help a clouded mind clear up, remove background noise, and focus intently on that which is at hand without judgment. Mindfulness meditation or mindfulness activities can be infused into all sorts of otherwise menial, daily things like breathing, eating, walking, et cetera.

Certainly, being "present" might sound to you as a goal that's rather abstract in nature, but the rewards that come with achieving that state are what you will be after. These can include reduced stress, emotional balance, emotional and mental resilience, clarity of mind, calmness, focus, concentration, and even physical benefits. As you can already see, a lot of those things translate well to your struggle against social anxiety. Imagine being able to block out all those negative thoughts and silence the inner voice that keeps telling you that you are threatened. Therefore, mindfulness is useful in curbing the symptoms of your SAD.

Mindfulness and associated meditative practices can be traced back to Buddhist traditions such as Zen and Vipassana. As such, it has been practiced in Buddhism's native lands in Asia for millennia. The practice started to gain ground and was popularized in the West during the 20th century. Like many other eastern practices such as yoga and other forms of meditation, mindfulness is something that gains more interest every year in the West.

Whether or not this popularity is due to perceived exoticism, meditation undoubtedly helps thousands, if not millions, of people every year. Apart from helping with stress-related issues, mindfulness is also used to alleviate symptoms of depression and even combat drug addiction. Furthermore, mindfulness isn't something that's only practiced by individuals on their own time in the West. In fact, mindfulness has been used in all sorts of environments, ranging from schools to prisons to all sorts of mental institutions.

The time around 1970 was something of a turning point for mindfulness because it started to gain more attention from mainstream psychology after that time. The research done on the subject since then has been rather extensive, although more of it is needed.

The success and usefulness of mindfulness in solving many of the problems we mentioned above have been documented and put to the test by science, with highly positive results. It has been found that mindfulness indeed helps with fighting various mental problems while also helping alleviate some simpler problems like excessive worry. Some research has even suggested that mindfulness is a useful tool in preventing mental health issues. There will have to be more research done in the future, but as things stand now, mindfulness is a proven technique, at least in a sizeable portion of its claims.

Apart from making you more present and focused, mindfulness should also help you get in touch with your emotions and become more aware of yourself as well. Because mindfulness is all about focusing on things without judgment, it won't lead to you ruminating on negative thoughts and making yourself feel worse. The idea is to just be more aware solely as a means of getting to know yourself better.

It's also worth mentioning that the process and the end goal of mindfulness can be achieved through various meditative exercises. Apart from being a practice, mindfulness is also a state of mind, and the roads that will lead there are various. Some people even hire personal trainers and other meditation experts to guide them through meditation exercises that can help achieve mindfulness. Still, you don't have to do that because mindfulness can be incredibly easy to practice.

Mindfulness also won't take up a lot of your time. If you so choose, you will be able to engage in mindfulness meditation for up to 40 or so minutes a day, but you can also spend far less time than that. It will be up to you to decide if you want to take up meditation sessions at home and really allocate that time and effort to turn it into a routine or if you want to do it on the fly. As we mentioned above, mindfulness works well with all sorts of daily activities and can fit seamlessly into your life, which is what makes mindfulness so accessible for all.

Mindfulness for Anxiety

So, how exactly do you go about practicing mindfulness, particularly taking social anxiety into account? It's not much more difficult than it sounds. Namely, it's all about choosing an object of focus and then using that object to ground yourself in the present. This object can be anything from your breathing pattern to a conversation that you might be having with someone.

Because one of the central ideas is non-judgment, the goal is to maintain a certain distance between yourself and the thing you are observing and focusing on, and especially between yourself and your emotional reactions. If you want to take some time out of your day and indulge in a meditation session to achieve mindfulness, you won't need any special equipment or experience. All you will need is some time and a quiet space where you won't be disturbed. You should choose a time of day when your schedule is the lightest and put your phone and other such distractions in another room or turn them off.

If you want to make things easier and more like advanced meditation, you can get yourself a cushion or a soft mat to sit on and assume a meditative pose. One common example is sitting on the ground with your legs crossed, and your hands are resting completely relaxed on your thighs. The important thing is to be relaxed and comfortable physically and to minimize distractions. Keep your back straight as well, and don't slouch, but don't make your back too stiff either. Again, there is really no set of rigid rules when it comes to mindfulness, and it can work even if you sit in a chair, as long as you are comfortable. The thing is that, if you're a beginner, getting comfortable and setting things up in this way can make for a better and more successful introduction to mindfulness.

You might also prefer to lower your chin a bit and turn your look downward, and you can also close your eyes if you wish. Closing your eyes can be useful if you're a beginner who has difficulty remaining concentrated because shutting your eyes will cut you off from anything that could get your mind wandering. Other than that, closing your eyes is not necessary. The clothes you wear are much more important when it comes to comfort. You shouldn't meditate in your jeans or other restricting clothes that keep reminding you that they are on you. Go with some loose and soft clothing.

The difference between mindfulness and many other kinds of meditation is that your objective is not to become calm or even shut off your mind. Again, the ultimate goal is just awareness in the full meaning of the word. Once you've positioned yourself the way you prefer and made yourself comfortable, you can start with the real, mental work of mindfulness.

The simplest object of focus that most beginners use is breathing. Don't try to control your breathing or breathe in a way that you think is correct. Just continue breathing as you would otherwise and observe - don't influence or analyze anything. Try to follow your breath by focusing on the physical sensations that each breath creates because this makes it easier to concentrate. Focus on things like the passage of air through your nostrils and the movements of your diaphragm and chest.

The idea is to try then and keep your attention solely on your breathing for as long as you can. With most people, especially beginners, their attention will inevitably start to shift to other things, usually their own thoughts. When this happens, you haven't failed as there is nothing to really fail at. Simply focus your attention back on the breathing, but do it gradually after a minute or so.

You must delay your re-focus because, as we mentioned above, it's important to distance yourself from your reactions. The same goes for when you start to feel an itch, or your leg gets uncomfortable. Don't react to these things right away. If your mind is particularly restless and keeps wandering, that's alright too. Rid yourself of all judgment and expectation. Your only goal is to try and be present while observing what your mind does with that.

Let the thoughts run their course without analyzing them and then try to refocus on your breath after a little while gently. Not passing any judgment toward your thoughts or the way your body reacts and not having expectations from your meditation is more difficult than it sounds. After a while, though, you will start to find it easier to stay focused for longer, and you will eventually start to feel more firmly grounded in the present moment instead of being subjugated to your mind and its scenarios and obsessions about the future or past. That's all there is to it when it comes to what mindfulness is.

Mindfulness on the Go and Additional Tips

We also mentioned that you don't really have to set aside a specific time and make mindfulness meditation a designated activity. Indeed, the alternative is to meditate on the go essentially. As we discussed, mindfulness can go hand in hand with many of the menial and seemingly mundane things you do daily. You can start to practice mindful eating, talking, exercising, walking, or even teeth brushing. There is almost no limit.

In that regard, you will use these things as the object of focus, just as you would use your breathing in the exercise we mentioned earlier. Ask yourself how often you are thinking about eating while you eat? That probably happens very rarely because you are so accustomed to it, and you tend to do it mechanically. On top of that, you have worries on your mind, and, often, your mind will wander toward those thoughts while you're having lunch.

Instead of wallowing in your thoughts, consider what you learned above and apply the same principles to your meal. Try to be aware of things like the taste, the number of chews you make, or the smell. A simple meal gives you much more opportunity to be mindful than a breathing exercise. Overall, just try to be more mindful of everything you do in daily life and always focus on the thing you are doing at that very moment. Even if you do just that, you will be practicing mindfulness. And that's the choice you have: You can formalize your meditation exercise and create a regimen for yourself, or you can introduce mindfulness into your regular life.

When it comes to your meditation if you continue to have great difficulties stopping your mind from racing when you sit down to meditate, and if these difficulties persist for a long time, there are ways to make things easier on yourself. One thing you can try is to make your meditation sessions shorter. We mentioned that you could engage in 40-minute sessions, but a mere 10-minute exercise can work just fine. When your sessions are long, and you consistently fail to focus, it might become difficult not to feel like you failed, so it's better to meditate in short bursts.

Another tool that everyone familiar with meditation will know is a mantra. Like meditation itself, mantras ("sacred sounds" or "sacred utterances") originate from India, and they are an integral part of many meditation exercises. One example is the Om mantra. In the simplest terms, this is a chant that meditators use to focus their mind and calm their thoughts. The nature of the "Om" sound is such that it can be chanter for a very long time and with varying intensity. If you are completely unfamiliar with mantras and can't understand how it sounds, there are many recordings of it on the Internet. A mantra is not just a sound to focus on and be mindful of; it also provides a certain vibration and sensation when chanted, which can assist meditation.

You can now probably see why mindfulness in all sorts of situations can be so powerful in suppressing your social anxiety. A misplaced focus has a lot to do with the onset of anxiety in each setting, and if you practice mindfulness while interacting with people, your mind can be much calmer.

You should also remember that social anxiety can be made worse by things like chronic stress, and you should know that there are many other exercises you can take up to reduce that stress and get a better command of your mind in general. There are many meditation courses, exercise groups, and personal trainers that can help you get much deeper into the world of meditation. You might find something that's perfect for you and can help change your life in many positive ways. There are also things like yoga, of course, which are constantly rising in popularity throughout the Western world.

Chapter Eight: Panic in Public Places – Ten Methods to Help You Relax

Before we get into some more ways in which you can combat your social anxiety long-term, we should also look at a few methods you can use to try and control your reactions on the spot. Although the idea behind most of these methods is just to soothe the symptoms, repeated use of some of them might also have a positive effect in the long term. Either way, whenever you succeed at overcoming an anxiety outbreak - even if it's just for a short while - you will feel strong and less helpless. Indeed, tackling your anxiety on the fly is a great way to take charge and lay the foundation for some more thorough psychological work and maintenance that you'll do later.

Of course, knowing how to subdue the symptoms at least when they arise can also make you more confident about getting into future social situations and breaking a cycle of avoidance. As already mentioned, exposure and gradual conditioning are some of the most important aspects of the struggle against SAD, so this added confidence can be a decisive boost.

Rationality Is Your Friend

As we discussed, anxiety is all about irrational fears, and rational thinking is indeed the antidote. Still, once anxiety takes over, it can be difficult to think rationally and get a grip on your racing thoughts, but you should always try to do it when your anxiety gets the better of you. Depending on how severe your anxiety is, you might not see any tangible results the first few times you try it, but after a while, you'll probably get the hang of it.

Your first step is to do your best to try and realize what's really happening. Consider your anxious reaction and try to focus on the fact that there is nothing to really fear and that you are not threatened. Your mind is fooled into perceiving a threat that isn't there, and it's triggering your flight-or-fight response for no good reason.

Furthermore, facts are your friend when you're trying to be rational. When you feel the onslaught of anxiety coming, try to focus only on the facts of the situation, *particularly positive facts.* If you're giving a presentation, for instance, and you're feeling anxious, try to think about how well-prepared you are and how knowledgeable you are on the subject. The chances are good that you're doing a great job, and the people you're presenting to are interested in the presentation, not your anxiety.

Breathe

As you know, breathing is highly relevant to anxiety. Therefore, breathing exercises are often used for all kinds of things like panic attacks, anger management, and outbreaks of anxiety. One of the simplest breathing exercises entails little more than slowing down your breathing and focusing on it.

Make sure that you are employing your diaphragm and not drawing shallow breaths. It's important to keep your breathing consistent and smooth. You should try to inhale for three to four seconds, hold the air in for three to four seconds, and then slowly exhale for the same amount of time. The point of the exercise is not to follow some golden rule about exhaling or inhaling for the exact, perfect amount of time. The idea is to keep your breathing deep and even so that your brain gets plenty of oxygen and to take your mind off the anxiety by focusing on your breathing instead.

It's important to control your breathing because it's often the first thing that suffers during an anxiety attack. Your breathing can become highly irregular, you may start to hyperventilate, or you might stop breathing altogether for a while. While breathing issues are a symptom on their own, disrupting the flow of oxygen to your brain can lead to all sorts of other symptoms of anxiety as well, such as tremors, dizziness, or even fainting. You should try to practice controlled and deep breathing at times when you're not anxious and then try to remember it when anxiety occurs again.

Interrupt Your Thoughts

When your mind starts racing, and your thoughts begin to get scary, the best thing to do is to break that negative train of thought as quickly as possible. One way to do this is with the so-called "3-3-3" rule. First, you should observe your surroundings and name the first three things you see; you can do this in your mind, if you want. Next up, scan around for three sounds and identify and name them as well. The last step is to move three parts of your body, for example: your ankle, fingers, and arm.

The idea is to distract your mind and give it something to do immediately. In fact, naming three visible things and three audible sounds might not be all that easy, depending on the environment you're in, so it can take some time and effort, which is good in terms of subduing the anxiety.

Of course, there are plenty of other things you can do to interrupt an outbreak of negative thoughts. This is highly contextual, of course, but nine times out of ten, there's something you can do to distract yourself. You can go for a little walk - even if it's just down the hallway - or you can get up and make some coffee, perhaps even clean up your desk. The important thing is to center your mind on something and get back into the moment.

Keep Busy

Indeed, keeping busy is one of the most important tips for dealing with anxiety on the fly. Don't sit around waiting for your mind to start noticing the people around you and getting ideas about what they may or may not be thinking about you. Get a jump on your own mind and focus on your work or whatever you're doing at that time.

It's a good idea to always keep some valuable distractions close by, including things like books or newspapers. If you're in a waiting room or on a crowded bus or train, reading is a very good way to focus your mind and forget about everyone around you. It's probably better than music, plus your ears won't be plugged. Of course, you can combine the two to shut off the world even more, if necessary.

Keeping busy is a good idea in general throughout your daily life, not just as a means of momentary distraction. Try and fill up your schedule with as many activities as possible and try to make them meaningful and fulfilling. The less time you spend sitting around and thinking negative thoughts, the weaker your anxiety will be. Heed this tip, especially when you find yourself anticipating an upcoming social situation. Instead of thinking about a million different scenarios where everything goes wrong, try to go for a walk or engage in a creative hobby instead.

Improve Your Posture

Like all people and a bunch of other creatures, you have a strong instinct to physically protect your vital organs when you're anxious and stressed out by a perceived threat. Usually, you won't even notice that you're doing it, but you will hunch over or cross your arms. This is a subconscious attempt to protect things like your heart and lungs, and it is an instinct left over from our cave-dwelling days.

Improving your posture can help calm you down and force your mind into accepting that there's nothing wrong and that nobody is about to attack you. Pay attention to the way you're standing or sitting next time you start feeling anxious. Try to stand up straight with your shoulders pulled back and your chest open and upward. Keep your feet apart, and don't cross your legs, especially if you're standing. Staring at the floor is another consequence of anxiety or worry, so you should try to correct that, as well.

Maintaining good is, of course, *not the cure* for social anxiety, but it's certainly something that can help. At the very least, you will project an image of confidence for others; when there are no symptoms to notice, you too will start to feel better and more peaceful.

Pull Yourself Back to Present

As you now know, social anxiety is often triggered by your notions of what's going to happen or might happen. It is the prospect of possible embarrassment or public humiliation that causes the problem, so you need to get your mind out of that fictional, future scenario and ground yourself in the present reality.

Imagine a scenario where you are late for a group meeting of some sort, and you must enter the room after everyone is already seated - a scary scenario for most sufferers of SAD. As you enter, you need to focus on the fact that you're just walking in and that being late isn't that big of a deal. Instead of obsessing over what others might be thinking or how you might get scrutinized, just focus on the task at hand. Your goal is to enter, sit, and participate, and that's all you must do and think about.

By focusing on what you're doing or are supposed to be doing, you will focus on something that's inseparable from the present moment. Furthermore, if you manage to convince yourself of the fact that you are not threatened, you might even be able to postpone your anxiety and your worries; promise yourself to address your problem later and analyze what you were worried about when you're at home.

Keep Company

If you are one of those people who have social anxiety but also happen to have a close friend or a few, you can try and keep them in your company when you feel that a situation might get difficult. Social anxiety tends to be much less intense or even non-existent when you surround yourself with people you are comfortable with.

Having a friend close by will give you something to focus on other than your anxiety. You can engage in small talk or similar interaction and keep your mind occupied by focusing on your companion instead of on your negative thoughts. Furthermore, your companion can divert the attention of others from you and make you feel less exposed. Sometimes, it's enough to be in another person's presence, but other times, it can help to tell them your problems and what you think might happen. You can try this approach next time you have an appointment or similar situation that you're anxious about, planning with your friend beforehand, agreeing to a few guidelines about dealing with an anxiety attack if it happens.

Talk to Someone About It

In this context, talking to someone about your anxiety means telling someone on the spot. If you have a friend with you, you can talk to them about how you are feeling now, but sometimes, there might also be an opportunity to talk to someone else. In fact, if you do it right, your anxiety might even be a topic that you can use to start up a conversation with a stranger.

We will look into the art of conversation and small talk later in the book, but for now, let's just say that, if you do it right, you can have a meaningful conversation about your anxiety while, at the same time, forgetting to feel anxious. It might sound counterintuitive when you're trying to forget about your anxiety, but talking about it can indeed be therapeutic. There's also a chance that you might end up talking to someone who has the same problem, and that sort of common ground can be the basis for friendship or other relationships. If you find yourself at a party or another similar social occasion, you can try and analyze the people around you and look for those who seem alone and isolated. The chances are that they are having the same issue as you are.

Think Positively

As we already discussed, defeating social anxiety has a lot to do with fighting your negative thoughts, and the importance of positive thinking can't really be stressed enough. Thinking positively is something you can try and do on the fly, not just some overall goal for your life that you need to work on over time.

You should try to relabel your negative thoughts and give them a positive spin. For instance, you can consider what we talked about earlier as your anxiety is natural and normal but misguided. Indeed, what's happening to you is that your natural survival instincts are misfiring and being misdirected – nothing more and nothing less.

It's also always a good idea to try and make things look funny in your mind. Take the people who you feel are giving you anxiety and try to imagine them in funny and unflattering circumstances. Even your anxiety itself can look funny if you try hard enough, since it is essentially an exaggeration, and exaggerations are usually an integral part of every good joke.

Focus on Others

The people responsible for your anxiety can be an endless source of distraction to help you take your mind off your anxiety. Keep in mind that the individuals who are completely confident and care-free - especially around strangers - are very rare. Whenever you meet someone, the chances are good that they are insecure about a few things. The chances are even better than they aren't giving much thought to judging and analyzing you and are, instead, thinking about the way *they appear to you.*

It's only natural to think about the impression you are giving when you meet someone, and this is how most people function. You should take advantage of that fact to help soothe your mind and take comfort in the realization that you aren't always scrutinized and judged every second of every interaction. Instead of looking at everything you are doing wrong (or *think* you are doing wrong), try focusing on the other person, for a change.

Chapter Nine: Social Confidence and Overcoming Shyness

While we have established that things like shyness are far from synonymous with social anxiety, you now know that they can certainly be connected. Shyness or perceived shyness can be symptoms of social anxiety, so there is common ground to consider between the two. Furthermore, social anxiety is also very likely to lead to low social confidence and damaged self-esteem, in general. As such, one approach to start curtailing your social anxiety is to try and boost your social confidence and learn how to carry yourself better in social situations.

With the necessary know-how and some effort, you might be able to fight through the anxiety and conduct yourself more confidently even when you are feeling anxious. Doing this can gradually get your mind used to the idea, and you might start to realize that your anxiety isn't that bad. Just managing to be functional despite your social anxiety is a great start. This isn't about faking confidence or just projecting an image, either. It's about actually boosting your confidence and overcoming a problem.

You should also note that the goal isn't to change your nature and force yourself into being extroverted when your personality is obviously that of an introvert. Not only would such efforts fail, but they would be a disservice to you and the way you really are.

Ultimately, you want to be the best possible version of yourself instead of something other people think you should be. It's that kind of self-acceptance that's one of the most important steps toward building your confidence.

How It Works

With all that said, if you have social anxiety, the chances are good that you have a problem with confidence as well. The two go hand in hand, and low social confidence or overall self-esteem can often be the core of the problem when it comes to SAD. As we mentioned, it also works the other way, as social anxiety that's brought on by other causes will usually inflict self-esteem issues on you sooner or later.

Nonetheless, confidence is something that can depend on a whole range of factors, and the causes tend to run deep and vary from one individual to the next. Everyone's story is different, and those stories are usually the place to look for clues as to the possible root of the problem. Confidence and self-image problems are often the results of past trauma, childhood experiences, and sometimes even genes. The first and most important thing to take away from that is that low confidence is not your fault in any way.

Self-esteem is quite possibly one of the most important things in life. It's a trait that can determine many outcomes in life and make or break you in countless situations. Confidence or lack thereof is a trait that's omnipresent and will be reflected in almost everything you do in life. Conversations, posture, laughter, thoughts, and even walking can all reflect an individual's level of confidence. What's more, humans are quite attuned to the variations in the self-confidence of others are adept at detecting whether someone is confident or not, so it's very difficult to hide.

The problems associated with low confidence go well beyond just social situations. A poor self-image is often at the core of self-esteem issues, which means that those who lack confidence tend not to like themselves very much. Apart from making you bad at parties, this can make you lack any will at all to improve any aspect of your life. It leads to complacency and a severe lack of motivation to the point where an individual might give up on happiness altogether. This is a vicious circle because self-improvement is often one of the more effective ways to boost confidence, but if you already think very poorly of yourself, it might get difficult to see the point of such efforts.

Social confidence - or confidence in social situations, to be exact - is just one of the more specific aspects of overall self-esteem, so the two are intimately connected. Confidence will make you more assertive and easygoing, but you will also be more stable and possess a certain firmness of character. Confidence is a shield that can protect you from many things that can otherwise sting. When it comes to criticism, for instance, folks with low self-esteem tend to react in one of two ways.

One part of the crowd will feel attacked and easily lash out in a highly defensive posture, even when the criticism is constructive and even friendly. The other part tends to be sensitive and to internalize every bit of criticism as evidence that they aren't good enough, leading them to be easily discouraged. When you are confident in yourself, your worth, and your abilities, you will stand firmly and, most importantly, you will have the ability to look at yourself with cold objectivity that allows you to consider criticism, analyze it, and use it to your advantage.

All in all, a lack of social confidence can often be just a symptom of a wider self-esteem problem. When you suffer from low confidence, it will show in many areas of your life and hinder your performance at work, in relationships, and elsewhere, with or without social anxiety.

What's very important to understand is that confidence is not something you can fake. Confidence is something that truly comes from within, and people are going to notice it, whether it's low or high. More importantly, trying to fake it will not help solve any of your problems, so there's little benefit even if you manage to fool someone. Unfortunately, the misconception that you can pretend to be confident is something that's still pervasive, and it is often offered as advice by friends and family.

Instead of applying a band-aid to the problem, you should address the underlying issues and seek a permanent solution. There are many ways to improve your overall confidence, including confidence in social situations. You can adopt new ways of thinking and engage in cognitive training, introduce changes into your daily life, exercise your social skills, and do numerous other things toward this end. Working on your confidence is one of the most important things you can do to fight your social anxiety and improve your life in general. Your level of confidence and self-esteem can often be the deciding factor in getting a job, a promotion, or building relationships. As such, your level of confidence can be a help or stand in your way toward happiness.

Methods to Boost Confidence

Let's consider some tips and methods that can help you boost your confidence over time. These tips concern both the way you think and the way you behave, and most of them will require you to give them a try and go through some trial and error. The most difficult part about boosting your confidence probably has to do with your thinking. Anyone can force certain behaviors with enough strength, but internalizing new principles and concepts that you aren't used to can require a whole new level of commitment.

Social Competence

As we mentioned, social competence and confidence are linked to your overall self-esteem, so this is something you should use to your advantage. We will take a more detailed look at social skills later, especially when it comes to having conversations, but for now, let's just say that the more you work on improving your social competence, the more confident you will get.

Social competence mostly revolves around getting people interested while also having an ability to listen truly and to make them feel like you're hearing them. As you start to improve your social competence by focusing on these skills, your self-image will start to improve. Research has confirmed as much on numerous occasions, giving a variety of explanations.

Of course, as someone who has social anxiety, you probably have a problem with these things, which is why you'll learn about improving your social skills later. The most important thing to note beforehand is the connection between confidence and successful interaction. Among other things, it has to do with social acceptance, which is one of the most important factors for confidence and overall wellbeing in humans, whether we want to admit it or not.

Body Language

We already touched upon body language in the previous chapter, and with good reason. Nonverbal communication is a major part of how we interact, so it's important to practice it just as much as speech and your thoughts. Proper body language that communicates confidence and comfort will make you appear confident, but, more importantly, studies have shown that you will eventually start to feel that way as well. This is particularly true for what some people call "power poses," which generally include open poses.

There are many other subtle and not-so-subtle aspects of body language you should note. For instance, it's always important to maintain eye contact and keep your handshakes firm, yet not too forceful. Of course, eye contact and staring are not the same. Try to keep eye contact at around 60% of the time when having a conversation; this helps you express interest and make people more comfortable, apart from just making you look confident.

As far as posture goes, aside from taking wide and open poses, make sure that you stay still and composed. Don't pace around, fidget, sway, or do other similar things that communicate nervousness. The three things (maintaining eye contact, open poses, firm handshakes) are essentially the three core aspects of confident body language.

Be Kind to Yourself

As you probably know, one of the key aspects of low self-esteem and social anxiety alike is that inner voice that may be constantly berating you. It's the voice that keeps tormenting you about the things you can't change, telling you how you're not good enough, or constantly comparing you to others.

If you're going to be more confident in yourself during social or any other situations, you need, first, to start treating yourself with more kindness. This doesn't mean not fixing the fixable, of course, but it does mean cutting yourself some slack. You should think about the way you would treat a close friend or a loved one. The chances are good that you would be supportive of them and try to console and encourage them when they do something wrong. Try to apply the same approach to yourself instead of always bringing yourself down.

A good way to do this is to start focusing more on your strengths, which you certainly possess. If you don't know what your strengths are, you should find out. When you fail at something, you should be able to remember that you're good at something else and that nobody can excel at everything.

Self-Improvement

Being kind to yourself while also always trying to improve in all important ways is the best combination. Self-improvement is a broad, all-encompassing term that can include all sorts of things like changes that you can introduce into your life. You can improve yourself by improving your health, your skills, your thoughts, your fitness, or anything else you can think of.

The important thing is the effect that self-improvement has on your confidence. Low self-esteem can sometimes stem from a real shortcoming or flaw that bothers us in ourselves, and most of the time, that is fixable. Every bit of progress you make toward improving an aspect of yourself will boost your confidence, even if you don't feel it at first.

To start with, you can focus on some very basic things like your diet or eliminating some of your bad habits. Most importantly: get to work becoming the best version of yourself that you can be. In fact, it's probably best that you start small since success in these seemingly unimportant things can give you the motivation to introduce bigger changes.

Self-Care

Self-improvement often technically involves a form of self-care as well. Fixing your diet, going to the gym, and getting healthier are certainly forms of self-care that are *in addition to* self-improvement. However, self-care isn't always about putting in some sort of work toward improving yourself.

Often, self-care simply means rewarding yourself and just learning to treat yourself better. As we mentioned, harsh self-criticism or even self-loathing often go together with low self-esteem. Therefore, it's important to replace some of that harshness with positivity and enjoyment, and this best in the form of rewards, which is why it goes along well with self-improvement.

Every time you go to the gym for a workout session, or you go through a day without indulging in a bad habit or meet whatever goal you've set, you should set aside some time for yourself in the evening. Think of any activity or reward you'd particularly enjoy and let yourself have it whenever you objectively earn it. It's incredibly easy to forget to give some time to ourselves, especially with the hectic schedules that many of us must endure every day. As soon as you start treating yourself better, though, your mind will have an easier time accepting that you're not that bad after all.

Practice

These were only some of the things you can do to improve your overall confidence and social confidence. When it comes to social confidence, the most important thing is to just get as much practice as possible. You need to get this practice despite any failures that you might experience. Even if the interactions don't go well, your brain will naturally get more and more used to people, the more you interact with them.

Just being out and about can be a form of practice of your social confidence, if you don't fall into some sort of avoidant routine. When they spend enough time with social anxiety, some folks will get so good at avoidance that they might spend a whole day outside running errands with next to no real interaction with anyone. Don't avoid the social situations that might be uncomfortable – seek them out. There is a good reason it used to be called social phobia. A lot of your struggle against SAD will require you to face your fears head-on and just start exposing yourself in order to harden.

Chapter Ten: Social Anxiety and Your Relationships

Thus far, we have mostly discussed social anxiety in circumstances that are highly socially dynamic and involve multiple people, particularly strangers and large social events or daily settings that involve strangers. In this chapter, we will look at how social anxiety relates to your relationships and how it can affect them. In fact, we will consider t the impact of social anxiety on human relationships, in general, and some tips on how to deal with it in these contexts.

It's certainly clear to you by now that social anxiety tends to occur mostly when strangers are involved. We mentioned earlier that socially anxious folks could often have a close friend or two whom they are comfortable with, and it's possible that you are in a similar situation. Still, social anxiety is something that can affect relationships, both potential and already existing ones. The greatest and most common difficulty is in forming new relationships, but there are ways in which your existing relationships – even those that you have cherished for years – can suffer.

Social Anxiety and Relationships

Of course, if social anxiety poses a problem for human relationships would be very intuitive, but there's a bit more to it than that. In the lives of most people, there exist relationships that predate the development of social anxiety. This primarily includes parents, siblings, and other family members, but it can also include childhood friends. These are the relationships we just mentioned when we talked about how socially anxious people can still be close to someone.

One way in which social anxiety can damage a pre-existing, functional relationship is by gradually driving a wedge between the two people. Imagine, for instance, a relationship such as a friendship or any other kind where the other person is highly sociable and outgoing while you are socially anxious and withdrawn. Apart from when you hang out one-on-one, you would mostly be inclined not to go out and socialize, turning down many invitations and gradually seeing less and less of that person. As close as they can be to us, our friends and loved ones can often be blind to our problems, especially subtle ones like anxiety. This is just one of the ways in which certain relationships can turn cold because of your anxiety.

Another problem that you might be well-aware of is that socially anxious people often find it difficult to discuss and express their feelings, *let alone articulate them.* This inability to communicate one's true feelings, including needs and desires, is what ends many - if not most – relationships, and the problem is especially pronounced with anxiety. It's not just that the anxiety has a direct effect on your ability to communicate. The issue is also in how your social anxiety has deprived you of meaningful contact and deeper interaction with others for so long. The inability to communicate and express emotions can simply be the result of a lack of experience.

According to some experts, this inability to express feelings and communicate on a deeper level is SAD's most damaging aspect when it comes to relationships. This was researched and supported by a 2018 Canadian study conducted at the University of British Columbia by Lynn Alden and other experts. The goal of this study was to challenge the traditional view that social anxiety should be treated by focusing solely on the reduction of avoidant behavior. The study postulated that the relationship deficit in social anxiety and the inability to express or articulate true feelings was just as important.

Yet another Canadian study - conducted at Western University by Christian Hahn - investigated the connection between social anxiety and relationship satisfaction too. As you would expect, the study found that relationship satisfaction was lower when social anxiety was involved. It was found that social anxiety was particularly detrimental for the trust and support in romantic relationships.

One of the main reasons for this is the sensitivity that social anxiety causes. This is the sensitivity toward criticism and fragile self-esteem, as we discussed earlier in the book. These things can get bad enough that even your romantic partner can start to appear like they are hostile, overly judgmental, and trying to humiliate you. Your partner might be trying to give you advice or help you in some way because they care, but to an anxious mind, help can often look like an attack. On top of that, the strong negativity bias and outright self-loathing that some socially anxious folks suffer from can make them deaf to positive feedback.

Beyond close friendships and romantic relationships, there are also relationships that you have with folks like your relatives. Relatives, particularly those from your extended family, exist in a sort of a grey area when it comes to closeness. On paper, they are to be considered close because they are part of the family, but in practice, most people see their relatives only periodically. This drives a wedge between you and them and can make family gatherings very stressful when you have social anxiety.

Furthermore, family gatherings can be such a circus of judgment and scrutiny that you might feel like you're being interrogated. Indeed, relatives always want updates, and they will pass their opinions on all sorts of things that concern you and your life. They will often compare you to others, ask you intimate questions, and really get under your skin - *even when they mean well.* Many people don't particularly enjoy that, let alone socially anxious folks! On top of that, it isn't uncommon for relatives to bring their friends or significant others to such gatherings, which means you can be forced to interact with strangers as well as members of your extended family.

With all that said, the most common way in which social anxiety affects relationships is still the way it diminishes your odds of establishing future ones. People who don't have social anxiety can go through break-ups, lose friends, get estranged from family, et cetera, but they will always be able to strike up a conversation and meet new people to fill the void. If you have both social anxiety and a close friend or a romantic partner in your life, then you know all too well how important and difficult to replace they are.

That's not to say that true friend is easy to come by or replace for anyone, but there is a whole other degree of hopelessness when your social anxiety keeps you down after a break-up or a loss of friendship.

Dealing with It

Obviously, the best way to deal with the damage that your social anxiety inflicts on your relationships is to deal with the social anxiety itself. What we have discussed and will continue to discuss after this chapter will help you in that regard, but you can still take steps to overcome anxiety-related issues in your relationships.

As you have probably gathered from what we talked about a little earlier, communication is paramount in romantic relationships. It's crucial in all human relations, of course, but romantic relationships are especially intimate, and, as such, they rest on the couple's ability to communicate on a deeper level than they would with anyone else in their lives. When two people function together, they communicate on all levels, verbal and nonverbal alike. They can weather through difficulties and misunderstandings because they know and understand each other, especially when it comes to all those quirks and weaknesses that people carry.

One of the most important things in this regard is to build and nurture trust. The only way you can strengthen that trust is by giving it a try. If you are intimate with someone and you care deeply about them, then you must trust them to make it work. You can start with some very simple things, such as honesty and the highest level of openness you can muster. Whenever you see a certain problem or anything bothers you, you must get on top of it as soon as you can and talk to your partner about it.

Don't let such issues lie dormant and fester under the surface. When things are bottled up, pressure builds, and those things that are left unsaid will often come back later and cause even more problems. They might also return as contempt, spite, and all manner of nastiness. All in all, every problem should be discussed and cleared up as soon as it arises. Not only will this solve more problems, but each time you do it, trust improves.

Communication that includes criticism should kept up to a certain standard. If you are sensitive to criticism and tend to be set off by such things, you should avoid being too critical of your partner, as well. Simply treat your partner with the same level of respect that you expect for yourself. Problems need to be talked about, *not yelled about.* Certainly, this is sometimes easier said than done, but with a bit of mindfulness and positive thought realignment, you should be able to control yourself - even when your partner can't.

That's really all there is to building trust: communicating in an effective and meaningful way while applying the golden rule. Once you feel that you trust your partner, but the problems associated with your anxiety keep coming back, you can try dealing with other issues.

You need to sit down and have an honest discussion with yourself concerning all the ways in which you could improve. To that end, consider all the things we have discussed, improving the way you think and all the other tips that have to do with behavior. Depending on your case, some of these things might help you, while others might not be as relevant. If you are unsure where to start, you can also talk to your partner about it, *if there is trust.*

Romantic relationships are a good place to be in when trying to beat your social anxiety. If you have both, you should also consider how lucky you are. For millions of people all over the world, being unable to find and establish such a relationship is the most excruciating aspect of their social anxiety. As such, you should consider your relationship as something that is already giving you a head-start.

When it comes to things like those pesky family gatherings we mentioned, the best way to deal with those situations is with the tips discussed before and after this chapter. Your best bet is to focus on that one relative or family member whom you are the most comfortable with. If you can relate to at least one person, that's an excellent, seamless inroad into a group, or at the very least, a conversation with such a person can help distract you.

With social anxiety and its relationship problems, friendships, and romantic relationships have a fair amount of common ground. Just like intimate relationships, true friendship entails trust, support, and communication. As such, a lot of what we have just discussed applies to friendships as well.

When it comes to romantic relationships or marriage, consider professional help. There is a specific type of cognitive-behavioral therapy, called CBT-R, wherein "R" stands for "relationships." This form of therapy for social anxiety with an emphasis on relationships has been found to work in studies such as the University of British Columbia study.

The availability of this approach might vary depending on where you live, but if all else fails, then it might be worth it to travel a bit to seek such help. There is nothing wrong with looking for help from an outside party, and it's a good idea to discuss it with your significant other, garnering their support and understanding which, in turn, provides you with a significant boost towards success.

Chapter Eleven: Small Talk and Other Social Skills for Introverts

Socially anxious individuals and most introverts can always benefit from learning about social skills that they would like to have. It's not always just about freeing yourself from fear and anxiety; though though that is certainly a great achievement, it probably won't magically make you adept at socializing overnight. This is especially true if the important developmental period in your life – the time when you were supposed to master these social skills – was marred by social anxiety and withdrawn living.

In that case, it might be necessary to catch up on some of that knowledge and learn some useful social skills to get you started in reclaiming your social life. It might be difficult at first, but once you get out there and see a couple of instances of success, things will often take a natural course, and you will be well on your way toward full recovery. We will take this chapter to discuss some of those useful social skills, especially those that relate to communication, and some additional tips to help you along the way.

Small Talk

We've already briefly mentioned small talk and how introverts, extroverts, socially anxious people, and others deal with it. What we didn't mention, however, is that despite how trivial it might be on the surface, small talk plays a very important part in the way human beings interact and communicate.

First and foremost, it provides a foundation for the interaction and familiarization between people because it plays an important part in our social rituals. Many acquaintances begin with chit-chat, and whether that acquaintance becomes something more will often depend on what happens during that initial stage exchanging pleasantries. As such, more advanced layers of communication and interaction can often depend on small talk. Being a basic and relatively simple social skill, small talk is also a great entry point for folks who wish to get back at the helm of their social life and start to practice their rusty or non-existent social skills.

Pleasant chit-chat is also a tool that can help calm you down in nervous social situations. As you know, many people will resort to small talk whenever they feel nervous or awkward in a situation. This is a very natural response, and it goes to show you how important it can be in terms of leveling things out and maintaining stability in social interaction. If you master it, small talk will always be that one card you can fall back on when things start to get anxious or awkwardly quiet.

It's also worth mentioning that small talk doesn't necessarily entail true conversations. Often, chit-chat will entail only a relatively quick exchange of remarks that will be just enough to get things moving along and make a situation more comfortable for the parties involved. In fact, you will mostly want to keep it that way as well. Don't go into too much detail or force conversations, especially conversations about serious topics.

As someone who struggles with social interaction, these short bursts of small talk, you can have will serve as a way for you to practice and get a foot in the door, so to speak. Just like mindfulness, it's something you should introduce into your daily life. You can think of situations like supermarket queues, going to the bank or DMV, or waiting for a train. All these situations will give often give you an opportunity to practice small talk. The best part is that they involve complete strangers whom you will never see again, so even if an embarrassing situation occurs, there will be no real consequence, and you can forget about it five minutes later!

In order to get enough practice, you will have to switch from waiting for small talk to *initiating it.* If you are unsure how you can initiate small talk in daily life, you should consider things like asking for directions or getting into situations with very active, large social gatherings - as scary as that might sound.

Consider a setting like a club or a rally of some sort. These situations involve a lot of strangers and a very high probability of interaction, but the important thing to note is your position therein. Namely, you will be nothing but a stranger in a sea of strangers, which can be a good thing. As counterintuitive as it sounds, crowds can be much less scary when you have SAD than one-on-one or being a stranger in a group of three to four people. There is simply so much attention going around in all directions that you will be protected by the statistics alone. It also means you can get to practice small talk with people who will forget all about it in five minutes if you cut off the interaction.

Overall, always keep in mind that small talk can easily spark a meaningful conversation and, eventually, friendship or even a romantic relationship. It might sound like a cliché, but it happens: people just click sometimes. If you stay positive and aren't forceful, you can rest assured that nothing bad came come from your efforts to engage in chit-chat with others. If someone reacts in a hostile or overly unpleasant manner, it won't be your fault.

When you strike up a conversation with someone agreeable, and you feel pleasant, small talk can go on for a longer time. In no time at all, you can find yourself moving from talking about the weather to really getting to know a person.

Advanced Communication

Being good at communicating with people is so much more than mastering small talk, of course. Knowing how to focus, listen, express, and present yourself with friendliness and style are all important skills to take communication beyond just small talk.

When it comes to communication with others, start with becoming a good listener. As someone who struggles with social interaction, you can gain a lot from just listening to people, regardless of who initiated the conversation. For one, when you let the other person do the talking, you are shifting the focus of the conversation and most of the thinking to them. This will give you some room to breathe, but it will also help you learn a thing or two about body language.

To be a good listener also means knowing how and when to react and nudge the conversation forward or even in the desired direction. You will need restraint, maybe more than you can anticipate. If your social anxiety has deprived you of interaction and meaningful conversations with people for a long time, you might be very eager to get talking, especially when you sense that the other person is beginning to take a genuine interest in you; it can be very tempting to talk on and on. To be a listener, you need to resist this urge and avoid inserting yourself into everything that the other person says.

Asking questions is an important part of keeping a conversation going. This is another reason why it's good to let the other person talk. The more they say, the more inspiration and material you will have for simple questions related to what they are talking about. You can insert these questions here and there to keep a conversation going along smoothly. Listening and gathering information will also help you make your questions engaging and original instead of mundane, making it look like you're only asking to seem nice or feign interest.

When a conversation starts running out of steam, and you need to give it a little push, you should ask questions that can't be answered with just a yes or a no. You should try and make those questions revolve around who, what, where, when, and why. Questions that start that way tend to give much more room for conversation and continuation of the discussion.

Most people love a good listener, so it's a good start if you want people to think you're a nice, pleasant person. Another disarming tactic is a simple compliment or two, being sure not to overdo it; make sure you only give sincere comments, and only when you really feel they are truly adequate. It's a very good way to set you up as friendly early in the conversation.

Eventually, you will also get into a situation where you will be the one who's supposed to lead a conversation. Expressiveness becomes very important if you are to get the message across while also keeping people interested and the conversation flowing. Try to be as descriptive- yet as simple and to-the-point - as possible when telling a story or describing anything.

In order to be more expressive and have your conversations go smoother, you might also want to try and create a script of sorts for how you want a conversation to develop. Of course, you can't script out the actual conversation with all its sentences, but you can write down a list or something similar, outlining your goals for when you have a conversation with someone. These goals can include certain topics you want to discuss, questions you want to ask, and other things. It's a good idea to know exactly what you want to accomplish by talking to someone.

Lastly, when it comes to expressing yourself, it's not all about the way you talk, either. Showing style in the way you clothe yourself, for instance, can leave a positive impression and impact the conversations you're having in a good way. In turn, this can also have a positive effect on your overall confidence, so the style can be very important indeed.

Overall, the most important thing is just to start conversing with people. Depending on your SAD and past record, it might be very difficult at first, but the illusion that conversations and strangers are scary is best dispelled by facing that fear head-on. As soon as you've had a few conversations, you will start to feel more at ease, especially if you started those conversations.

Other Tips

In general, if you aren't overly trusting, the best way to approach people is to consider everyone a potential friend whom you just didn't find yet. Keep in mind that there are many other people you could run into who also suffer from social anxiety. Your similar experiences can be a conversation topic and a starting point for a great friendship, but it can also make it exceptionally difficult to get things going. Therefore, it's important to be friendly, pleasant, and smile whenever you can. That's not to say that you should fake a smile to impress someone, quite the contrary – an earnest smile can make anyone feel more at ease when they interact with you.

One important thing you can do in the way of improving your social skills is to observe and learn. You will inevitably come across people who are confident and very adept at socializing, and you will be able to learn a lot just by observing them. When it comes to social skill and confidence, there are some things that can hardly be described with words, so you will have to learn them on the fly. When you see someone who socializes with ease, take note of their body language and the way they speak. You will see many of the tips you've learned in this book come seamlessly into a real-life scenario.

It's important to understand that your goal isn't to fundamentally change who you are. If you are introverted, it's only natural not to be the life of the party and a master of social skills. Your goal is to rid yourself of all fear and to be able to function when social situations do arise, not to become suddenly ultra-sociable. It's perfectly fine to skirt being the center of attention, staying reserved, and not going out every night. If this is who you are, so be it, and you should wear your nature with pride.

Once you defeat your social anxiety and become more confident, your introversion can become something that's appealing. This is true both for men and women. Introversion can give certain people an interesting aura of mystery and enigma that attracts people. The old cliché about being yourself still holds true and will continue to be so.

When you start to like yourself, and when your fear of judgment has subsided, you will find that other people will have an easier time liking you, too.

Another important tip when you're trying to improve your social skills is to do your best to make your strengths and virtues come to light. Take a moment to consider what these strengths of yours are. Maybe you are good at listening to people and giving them advice, or perhaps you are very knowledgeable about certain interesting topics. Whatever it is, try to make it come to the spotlight instead of trying to pretend that you're an extrovert to fit in. That would be the road toward being a show-off - and nobody likes that.

Remember that, as an introvert, you still need that downtime you spend alone to recharge. When you are trying to hone your social skills, you should always approach situations with a fresh and eager mind. If you force yourself into too much social interaction in a short span of time, you might get to feeling burned out, and that will make interaction much more difficult and disheartening.

As you can see, there really isn't all that much to it. You must practice and keep on practicing; your social skills will eventually have to come back to you. Even if you throw yourself back into society abruptly, shock your mind and body, and encounter a few abysmal failures, it will still count as practice. Social skills are like riding a bicycle in that you have it in you, but you just need to commit to it and not get discouraged - even if you fall flat on your face. The more you talk to people, the easier it will get, and - most importantly - you will get to see how little there is to fear.

You will also see just how many other people have a whole range of problems that they struggle with, and that can do more to make you feel less isolated than the interactions themselves. You will quickly realize that strangers aren't these perfect beings who have it all figured out, who all belong to some club that you need to join while they judge your every move. A million people will have a million different struggles; getting to learn about them will be one of the more fascinating aspects of your journey.

Chapter Twelve: Breaking Out of Your Comfort Zone

As you have probably gathered in the course of this book, beating your social anxiety will require you to traverse beyond your comfort zone many times and in many ways. This can entail copious amounts of fear, stress, frustration, and failure, but all of it will be necessary if you are to rewire your brain and rid yourself of your fears permanently.

Given enough time, your social anxiety can completely convince you that you are comfortable in isolation and that you really don't have to change anything. This illusion is one of the more dangerous aspects of social anxiety, and it can exist for a long time. At some point, though, the illusion is broken when you realize how much you have missed out on and how many areas of your life have come to be affected by it. Since you are reading this book, the chances are good that this has happened to you.

What Is Your Comfort Zone?

Perhaps the fact that this is an illusion is what makes the term "comfort zone" a bit inaccurate too. Namely, a state that you were conditioned to be in because of your fears might not qualify as a very comfortable one, once you take a closer look at least. There is comfort, and then, *there is complacency.*

Indeed, the difference between the two is significant yet often overlooked. Most people don't make that distinction, and it can lead to them being misunderstood, particularly when they give advice to introverts. As we discussed, introverts such as yourself are naturally more comfortable in calm environments and among few friends, and there is nothing wrong with that. As such, when you are advised to get out of your comfort zone, what's meant is not that you need to stop being you. Instead, the idea is to get out of what some people call the "complacency zone."

The complacency zone is the illusion we mentioned earlier. It is a place where our fear and anxiety force us to go and hide in order to avoid having to deal with the discomfort of those situations that we dread. When you find that you have established a daily routine around that fear and constructed your days in a way that allows you to avoid social situations, you have settled in the complacency zone. Has your social anxiety made you order food instead of going out to get it yourself? Do you find that you often come up with weak excuses not to go out when a friend calls you?

It's that avoidance that keeps your social anxiety going strong and getting stronger over time. And because you think you are avoiding fear and stress, you begin to think that you are comfortable in this avoidance. In reality, though, you are becoming complacent and are accomplishing nothing but allowing what is essentially a curable disease to take hold of you and control your life.

In fact, you're not even avoiding your fear, as much it as might feel that way. Your fear always continues to be present, and it continues to rule your life even though you've minimized the amount of anxiety you feel. As such, your complacency zone is a place where you accomplish nothing and are, in fact, probably making things worse. This is a status quo that you don't want to uphold if you wish for things to get better in a meaningful way. You and your social anxiety aren't a unique case of this either. Plenty of people are stuck in some sort of complacency zone that's relevant to their problems.

The way you think and behave can be indicative of whether you are stuck in this zone. For instance, do you often find that you tend to put off solving certain problems, preferring instead to pretend like the problems aren't there? A complacency zone also comes with a whole lot of rationalization where you might be looking for excuses and seemingly rational explanations for your avoidance and inactivity. Your complacency and fear might make you turn down an offer to meet up with a friend, but you might not tell yourself that. Namely, when we are stuck in this situation, it's easy to come up with a million seemingly rational explanations, such as that we were tired or too busy when we know deep down that this isn't true.

As you can see, there isn't a whole lot of "comfort" that goes into any of this, just self-delusion and stagnation. Another reason why it's important to understand the difference between this and a "comfort zone" is that you want to rely on your strengths in the struggle against social anxiety. For instance, when an introvert gets to thinking that he or she is supposed to act like an extrovert in order to leave their perceived comfort zone, that person will set themselves up for failure.

You have enough on your plate with your social anxiety, so it's not always a good idea to put yourself in situations that don't agree with your personality on top of that. As an introvert, it might be better for you to try and practice your social skills in situations where your innate introvert strengths can shine. Think of things like your concentration, introspection, and other things you're good at.

If we use these definitions and consider the difference between comfort and complacency, it becomes clear that your actual comfort zone is not necessarily a bad thing. Keeping all this in mind, consider the nature of extroverts for a moment. Being surrounded by lots of people and getting a lot of interaction is what we would consider an extrovert's comfort zone. Of course, people don't tend to encourage extroverts to get out of this particular "comfort zone," and extroverts are encouraged instead. As such, misguided advice ends up encouraging introverts to quite literally leave their natural "comfort zone" and then pretend to be comfortable in that of extroverts.

With all that said, it's true that most people simply use the term "comfort zone" as a synonym for what we just described as the complacency zone. Now that we've cleared up the important difference and real meaning of both, we will do the same from here onward to keep things simple.

Much of what we've discussed in this book already entails breaking out of your comfort zone. Starting conversations, taking up meditation, addressing the troublesome thoughts you carry in your mind, and a few other things we mentioned can all be uncomfortable when you have SAD. As with many other things in life, the most difficult part for many people is just to get started.

Avoidance can get so familiar, and your mind can get so used to it that you completely forget what it's like to be in any other state. It might seem unbelievable to those of you with only mild social anxiety, but some folks have indulged their fear and been avoidant for so long that even the most basic of interactions can appear impossible. That's why you might start thinking that you are more comfortable staying inside and cutting the world off.

By breaking out of that idea of comfort and facing your fears, you will find that your mind might just as easily get accustomed to interaction as it did to isolation. Even when struggling with personality disorders, humans still have an incredible capacity to adapt and get used to new situations, especially when they are routine. If you find the strength to make those initial steps, you will find that *anything is possible.*

Breaking Out

So, how do you get out of your comfort zone? It will generally entail assertiveness and decisive action or, in a word, boldness. Still, you can be methodical, systematic, and gradual with how you depart from your comfort zone. There are numerous strategies, tips, and changes you can try out, particularly when it comes to social anxiety.

Preparing for the First Step

This doesn't mean preparing to make a movie in each moment when you're already in a certain situation. It means preparing your mind and body during your days when the moment to act comes. You can prepare yourself to leave your comfort zone in many ways, some of which we've already discussed. Self-improvement is certainly one example. It can help many folks if they are fit, for instance, so picking up a workout regimen and getting yourself in shape can always make it easier to break out of your socially anxious comfort zone.

It's also important to get some things straight with yourself. For one, consider what that most problematic part about yourself, which you want to change, is. Try to pinpoint the exact behavior that you want to stop in the future. This can be something very simple and small just to get you started. Think about a certain thing that you do to indulge your social anxiety, such as avoiding talking on the phone. Pick any individual piece of your avoidant behavior and focus on breaking the cycle the next time an opportunity arises. The moment you act and say no to your avoidance, even in the simplest way, will be the moment you begin your new life.

Create a Plan of Action

Something else that's useful is to have reasons for doing what you do. That way, if the going gets tough or you get cold feet, you always have those reasons to fall back on. Always keep your reasons and your overall goals in mind, using them as a source of energy.

Furthermore, it's good always to have a relatively detailed and solid plan for the things that you want to do. Are you intending to break out of your comfort zone by applying for a new job and going to the interview? In that case, make a plan that includes all the things you want to say how you are going to present yourself, and all the other parts that go into it. You should plan for when things go south, such as if the interviewers ask you a trick question or expose your weaknesses.

Without obsessing over how you are going to get anxious, you should make a clear plan and a backup plan so that you're never caught in the headlights. Unexpected turns can leave you stumped and trapped in an anxious cycle. The objective of being prepared is not just to succeed but also to deal with failure and pick yourself up for that next attempt. Wherever you go, venture out with a plan.

Adjust Your Expectations

First and foremost, you should, of course, expect lots of discomfort and brace yourself for numerous failures, just in case. We did mention that taking the first step is most important, but that doesn't mean you should expect things to just magically come together as soon as you take a step in the right direction.

Try to consider all the possible ways in which a situation can go, writing those scenarios down. This can often have a calming effect because it makes things seem less scary than they were in your head. Furthermore, we are not talking about obsessively worrying about a scenario; simply try to be as objective as possible, thinking of a few ways that your venture outside the comfort zone can go. The purpose of that is to show you that even the worst scenario is probably harmless and won't have any lasting ramifications, giving you more motivation to do it.

The most important thing is not to have expectations that are too high. In fact, that's more important even than having them be too low. Don't set yourself up for disappointment because that can be more discouraging than any bad scenario you can think of. Consider both the good and possible bad outcomes and try to change your perspective from worrying to curiosity. Try to make yourself simply curious to see what happens when you step out of that zone.

Don't Think Too Much

Opportunities to break out of your comfort zone can often appear out of nowhere. You might find yourself outside, just going about your day, when suddenly, there is an opportunity to interact with someone and establish meaningful contact. Of course, these chances are especially common when you go out for the night, for instance.

If you decide that approaching someone and starting a conversation is your preferred way of breaking out of your comfort zone, you should apply something that some folks refer to as the "three-second rule." This rule applies to all sorts of ways to break out of comfort zones, not just in social situations. It simply prescribes to wait no more than three seconds before acting.

The goal is not to let your mind fall into its old pattern of overanalyzing and panicking over a million ways in which you can embarrass yourself. If you see someone you want to talk to, simply tell yourself that this is the opportunity you've been waiting for, not something to fear, and then make a move. Certainly, this is easier said than done, and it might take some practice before you succeed, but the results can be incredible. When you don't give your fearful mind enough time to shut you down, you might quickly find yourself in a pleasant conversation, realizing how little there was to fear. This is one of the best ways to strike against social anxiety.

Stop Being an Observer in Your Life

Ask yourself one simple question: Do you want to take charge and play an active role in your life, or would you rather be a bystander to your own story? There are only a few things that can lead you down a road of passivity the way social anxiety can. This disorder wants you to shut yourself off and let your life pass you by. It wants you to sit at home, adopt a passive existence where you just wait for things to happen instead of making them happen.

As comfortable as that might appear to your conditioned mind, it won't work out in the end. To get anywhere in life, you first need to start moving, and it doesn't matter how small those initial steps are, *as long as you make them.* If you see people doing the things you want to do, ask yourself what's really stopping you. One of the most important things you have learned from this book is that social anxiety is something you can and must beat on your own. It's not a problem that others can solve for you. You must stop being the audience to your own life and start assuming the main, active role that was always meant for you.

Conclusion

As you can see, your social anxiety is a burden you can throw off over time. Although nobody's story is quite the same, your first source of comfort can be the realization that your problem is a very common one. What's also entirely likely is that there are many, many people out there whose social anxiety is much worse than yours. Nonetheless, even they can overcome it, and they do, often completely on their own.

If you do have support from a friend or beloved family member, though, that's even better. You should talk to them about your problem, especially if they are extroverted and don't have any such issues. Having those that are close to you understand what you're going through can be incredibly encouraging, but it can also make your life and your recovery easier.

You also shouldn't refrain from seeking professional help from a psychiatrist or therapist. You can always schedule a session at least as a means of diagnosis and to have a little conversation. It never even occurs to many people that they could seek out such help, much less that it could help them, but they are usually wrong. Therapists can be incredibly adept at getting to the root of your problems, and you might be surprised by the help they can provide in a short period of time. What's more, you might find that they are quick to catch on to things that you thought nobody would ever understand.

All in all, your time has come to a stop despairing and especially to stop letting this disorder run your life and take the joy right out of it. You now know that you don't have to live this way and that it only takes a bit of effort and some patience on your part. With an informed and positive attitude, you might turn into a whole new person!

Resources

https://www.psycom.net/social-anxiety-disorder-overview

https://adaa.org/understanding-anxiety/social-anxiety-disorder

https://www.webmd.com/anxiety-panic/guide/mental-health-social-anxiety-disorder#1

https://socialphobia.org/social-anxiety-disorder-definition-symptoms-treatment-therapy-medications-insight-prognosis

https://www.mayoclinic.org/diseases-conditions/social-anxiety-disorder/symptoms-causes/syc-20353561

https://www.youtube.com/watch?v=BcRobzrfc98

https://introvertdear.com/news/anxious-introverts-fears/

https://www.psychologytoday.com/us/blog/the-secret-lives-introverts/201805/15-signs-anxious-introvert

https://www.wisebread.com/7-social-situations-all-introverts-fear

https://www.healthline.com/health/how-to-calm-anxiety#3

https://www.verywellmind.com/managing-panic-disorder-in-public-2584185

https://www.healthline.com/health/mental-health/panic-attacks-in-public#4

https://www.webmd.com/mental-health/features/ways-to-reduce-anxiety

https://verilymag.com/2018/12/signs-of-social-anxiety-social-anxiety-disorder-anxiety-introvert

https://www.youtube.com/watch?v=n5Xsk6vwzYY

https://www.huffpost.com/entry/difference-social-anxiety-introversion_n_5adf5e6de4b07560f3961226

https://www.melbournechildpsychology.com.au/blog/distinguishing-behaviours-the-difference-between-shyness-introversion-and-social-anxiety/

https://www.quietrev.com/the-4-differences-between-introversion-and-social-anxiety/

https://www.promisesbehavioralhealth.com/addiction-recovery-blog/introvert-shy-socially-anxious-whats-the-difference/

https://introvertdear.com/what-is-an-introvert-definition/

https://www.verywellmind.com/signs-you-are-an-introvert-2795427

https://psychcentral.com/blog/treating-social-anxiety-with-meditation-and-mindfulness-training/

https://www.verywellmind.com/meditation-for-social-anxiety-3024211

https://missionbe.org/faq/?gclid=Cj0KCQiAvJXxBRCeARIsAMSkAppB8mkjiygV7Gu4HMMpnF8FK5YnBC81SJpET4pbC7TbR2JtF_U6-L0aAkgPEALw_wcB

https://www.mindful.org/meditation/mindfulness-getting-started/

https://www.alustforlife.com/soul/you-are-alive/10-mindfulness-tips-to-help-you-live-a-more-peaceful-life?gclid=Cj0KCQiApaXxBRDNARIsAGFdaB_N1hDQZTikREC_dw6tnrGUh4hDNxke05cEVuaeSm6sTM0zNVGYXrwaApweEALw_wcB

https://www.youtube.com/watch?v=ld_QpsD0qpk

https://www.mindful.org/mindfulness-how-to-do-it/

https://www.youtube.com/watch?v=xsCxltuzmDI

https://www.youtube.com/watch?v=CjsZfYjaTUQ

https://www.elitedaily.com/p/how-introverts-can-make-small-talk-less-painful-more-meaningful-according-to-experts-8917603

https://www.lifehack.org/articles/lifestyle/7-epic-strategies-for-introverts-by-introverts-to-ignite-your-social-skills.html

http://elitemanmagazine.com/10-tips-to-becoming-more-social-as-an-introvert/

https://www.youtube.com/watch?v=Jv_Qjis_ZXo
https://www.youtube.com/watch?v=xIE_w0QLyiE
https://www.youtube.com/watch?v=2yRVP9PHnEE
https://www.wikihow.com/Be-Socially-Confident
https://www.lifehack.org/372358/5-ways-start-building-social-confidence-today
https://thriveglobal.com/stories/comfort-zone-or-complacency-zone-please-stop-scaring-introverts/
https://nationalsocialanxietycenter.com/2018/02/16/overcoming-social-anxiety-choosing-step-outside-comfort-zone/
https://herpaperroute.com/get-out-of-your-comfort-zone/
https://www.psychologytoday.com/intl/blog/cutting-edge-leadership/201405/introversion-5-strategies-pushing-out-your-comfort-zone
https://www.youtube.com/watch?v=3jy-44L7_bo
https://www.youtube.com/watch?v=cmN4xOGkxGo
https://www.health.harvard.edu/blog/do-i-have-anxiety-or-worry-whats-the-difference-2018072314303
https://www.psychologytoday.com/us/blog/the-squeaky-wheel/201603/10-crucial-differences-between-worry-and-anxiety
https://www.verywellmind.com/fear-and-anxiety-differences-and-similarities-2584399
https://www.psychiatry-uk.com/anxiety-explained/
https://www.psychologytoday.com/us/blog/science-choice/201812/anxiety-vs-fear
https://www.goodtherapy.org/blog/psychpedia/trigger
https://www.verywellmind.com/which-situations-trigger-anxiety-3024887
http://overcomingsocialanxiety.com/common-social-anxiety-triggers/
https://www.youtube.com/watch?v=mmPMwYHtoD4
https://www.helpguide.org/articles/anxiety/social-anxiety-disorder.htm

https://lifehacker.com/what-anxiety-actually-does-to-you-and-what-you-can-do-a-1468128356

https://www.psychologytoday.com/us/blog/wander-woman/201507/5-steps-managing-your-emotional-triggers

https://www.inc.com/nate-klemp/try-this-neuroscience-based-technique-to-shift-your-mindset-from-negative-to-positive-in-30-seconds.html

https://www.psychologytoday.com/us/blog/women-s-mental-health-matters/201509/7-ways-deal-negative-thoughts

https://www.verywellmind.com/what-are-negative-automatic-thoughts-3024608

https://www.psychologytoday.com/us/blog/the-mindful-self-express/201708/3-negative-thinking-patterns-avoid-what-do-instead

https://www.psychologytoday.com/intl/blog/fulfillment-any-age/201806/is-social-anxiety-getting-in-the-way-your-relationships

https://psychcentral.com/blog/you-can-stop-social-anxiety-from-ruining-your-relationships/

https://www.psychologytoday.com/intl/blog/fulfillment-any-age/201501/6-ways-get-more-comfortable-others-and-yourself

https://shynesssocialanxiety.com/nervous-around-relatives/

https://www.verywellmind.com/managing-social-anxiety-disorder-at-work-3024812

https://www.anxiety.org/if-social-anxiety-disorder-affects-your-romantic-relationships

Made in the USA
Las Vegas, NV
28 January 2021